Wildlife Collector Plates

for the Scroll Saw

by Rick and Karen Longabaugh

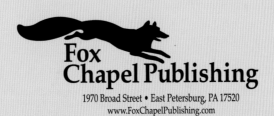

Fox
Chapel Publishing

1970 Broad Street • East Petersburg, PA 17520
www.FoxChapelPublishing.com

Alan Giagnocavo
Publisher

Peg Couch
Acquisition Editor

Gretchen Bacon
Editor

Troy Thorne
Cover Design & Layout

Bibliographical Note
Wildlife Collector Plates for the Scroll Saw is a revised and expanded republication of *Wildlife Scrollsaw Collector Plates*, originally published in 1999. This edition of the work includes expanded instructions for getting started along with full-color photos and a full-color gallery of finished projects.

ISBN-13: 978–1–56523–300–3
ISBN-10: 1–56523–300–X

Publisher's Cataloging-in-Publication Data

Longabaugh, Rick.

    Wildlife collector plates for the scroll saw / by Rick and Karen Longabaugh. -- East Petersburg, PA : Fox Chapel Publishing, c2006.

        p. ; cm.

        ISBN-13: 978-1-56523-300-3
        ISBN-10: 1-56523-300-X
        Includes index.

        1. Wood-carving--Patterns. 2. Wood-carving--Technique. 3. Wildlife wood-carving--Patterns. 4. Jig saws. I. Longabaugh, Karen. II. Title.

TT199.7 .L668 2006
736/.4--dc22   0604

Printed in China
10 9 8 7 6 5 4 3 2 1

To learn more about the other great books from Fox Chapel Publishing,
or to find a retailer near you, call toll-free 1-800-457-9112 or visit us at
www.FoxChapelPublishing.com.

Note to Authors: We are always looking for talented authors to write new books in our area of woodworking, design, and related crafts. Please send a brief letter describing your idea to Peg Couch, Acquisition Editor, 1970 Broad Street, East Petersburg, PA 17520.

TABLE OF CONTENTS

Rick and Karen Longabaugh started The Berry Basket and Great American Scrollsaw Patterns—their family-owned online and mail order company, specializing in unique and useful scroll saw patterns and accessories—in the fall of 1990. What began as one set of collapsible basket patterns became a complete line of full-size woodworking patterns and hard-to-find accessories.

Rick has been featured on the popular PBS show *The American Woodshop* with Scott Phillips and also on the cover of *Popular Woodworking* magazine. Many of their unique projects have been published in a number of woodworking publications, including *Wood* magazine, *Creative Woodworks & Crafts*, *Popular Woodworking*, *The Art of the Scroll Saw*, *Scroll Saw Workshop*, and Patrick Spielman's *Home Workshop News*.

INTRODUCTION

Since the early 1900s, numerous companies have offered what they call "Collector Plates." These plates, generally made from porcelain or ceramics, are produced in "Limited Edition" quantities. They offer subjects and designs ranging from wildlife and Victorian floral to family trees and children's fairy tales. These have proven to be very popular worldwide—hence, our idea to create a unique and easy way to scroll collector plates in your shop at home. This collection of wildlife patterns is a wonderful way to display your scroll saw talents and add beautiful decor to any room in your house. These projects make a beautiful display whether hung individually on your wall or in groups. We have even included a design for a plate stand so you can easily display them on a shelf, desk, or dresser. Any of these designs would make a wonderful present that would surely be treasured for years to come.

GETTING STARTED

The following scroll saw tips and techniques are intended to get you started and on your way to scroll saw success. You will find these techniques helpful in completing the projects in this book as well as other scroll saw projects.

SAFETY TIPS

Always keep safety in mind as you are working. Here are some general safety guidelines to take into consideration before you begin.

- Use glasses, goggles, or similar equipment to protect your eyes.

- Remove any loose clothing or jewelry before you operate your saw.

- It is always a good idea to work in a well-ventilated area. Consider using a mask, an air cleaner, a dust collector, or any combination of these to protect your lungs from fine dust.

- Be sure that your work area is well lighted.

- Keep your hands a safe distance away from the blade.

- Don't work when you are tired or unfocused.

COPYING THE PATTERN

The patterns contained in this book are intended to be your master patterns. We recommend making photocopies of the project pieces and then using a repositionable spray adhesive to adhere them to your workpiece. This method of transfer is easier, less time-consuming, and far more accurate

than tracing. Using a photocopier will also allow you to enlarge or reduce the pattern to fit the size of wood you choose to use. Please note that some photocopy machines may cause a slight distortion in size, so it is important to use the same photocopier for all of the pieces of your project and to photocopy your patterns in the same direction. Distortion is more likely to occur on very large patterns.

All of the plate patterns in this book are full-size and will make finished projects of approximately 9" diameter for the larger plates and 7"diameter for the miniplates. If you would like to enlarge these projects, the following chart will help you get started:

Large Plates		Mini-Plates	
% Enlargement	Size	% Enlargement	Size
100%	9" diameter	100%	7" diameter
116%	10" diameter	116%	8" diameter
135%	11¾" diameter	135%	9" diameter

PREPARING THE SURFACE

For most projects, it is best to sand the workpiece prior to applying the paper pattern and cutting the design (see **Figure 1**). Once you've cut the design and removed the paper pattern, it may be necessary to lightly sand off any glue residue remaining, along with any "fuzz" on the bottom side.

TRANSFERRING THE PATTERN

Using a repositionable spray adhesive is the easiest and quickest way to transfer a pattern to your workpiece after photocopying it. (These adhesives can be found at most arts and crafts, photography, and department stores. Pay special attention to purchase one that states "temporary bond" or "repositionable.")

Start by setting up in a well-ventilated area. Lightly spray the back side of the paper pattern, not the wood (see **Figure 2**). Allow it to dry only until tacky—approximately 20 to 30 seconds. Then, apply it to the workpiece, smoothing out any wrinkles if necessary.

One of the most common problems with using repositionable spray adhesive for the first time is applying the right amount onto the back of the pattern. Spraying too little may result in the pattern's lifting off the project while you are cutting. If this occurs, clear Scotch tape or 2" clear packaging tape can be used to secure the pattern back into position. Spraying too much will make it difficult to remove the pattern. If this occurs, simply use a handheld hair dryer to heat the glue, which will loosen the pattern and allow it to be easily removed.

SELECTING THE MATERIALS

Selecting the type of material that you will use is very important for the final outcome of your project. All of the projects in this book have been designed so that hardwoods, plywoods, or a combination can be used to create your work of art.

Hardwoods offer a wide variety of species, colors, and grain patterns; however, they are more time-consuming to cut, require more sanding, are more likely to warp, and are more expensive to use (see **Figure 3**). Generally, any of the domestic or imported varieties will work well—ash, maple, walnut, oak, birch, mahogany, cherry, and hickory are just a few of the common types.

Plywoods, on the other hand, are less expensive, require less sanding, and come in a variety of standard thicknesses. They also are less likely to develop cracks or to warp. We do, however, recommend that you use top-grade plywood without voids, such as the Baltic and Finnish birches.

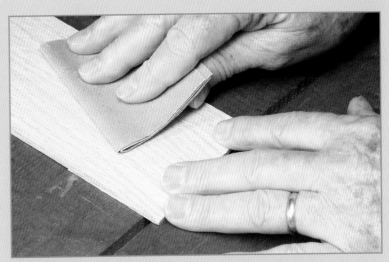

Figure 1. Be sure to sand the workpiece before applying the pattern. You may also want to sand the wood lightly once you have cut the design and removed the pattern to eliminate any "fuzz" and to get rid of any glue residue.

Figure 2. Use "repositionable" spray adhesive to adhere your patterns to the wood. A simple glue box, made from a common cardboard box, helps to confine the adhesive.

Figure 3. Hardwoods offer a variety of colors and grain patterns that can enhance your projects. Shown here from left to right are catalpa, red oak, cherry, birch, black walnut, white oak, mahogany, and American aromatic cedar.

Skip Tooth Blades

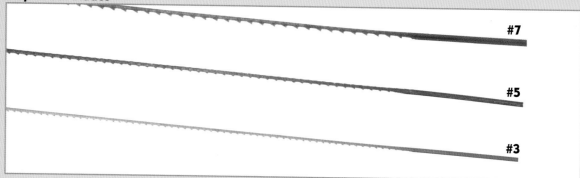

#7

#5

#3

Figure 4. Skip tooth blades can be good blades for a beginning scroller. Pictured here from bottom to top are skip tooth blades #3, #5, and #7.

SELECTING THE BLADE

There are many opinions regarding which blade to use, depending on which type and thickness of material you choose and on how intricate the design in the project is. The more time you put into scrolling, the more your choice of which blade to use will become personal preference.

For the beginning scroller, we recommend skip tooth blades, but be sure to experiment and find the blade that suits you best (see **Figure 4**). We also offer the following blade size guidelines to get you started:

Material Thickness	Blade Size Recommended
¹⁄₁₆" to ¼"	#2/0, #2, or #3
¼" to ½"	#5 or #7
½" to ¾" or thicker	#7 or #9

Figure 5. One way to check if your table is square to your blade is to use a small square. Place the square next to the blade and adjust the table as necessary until the blade and the square are parallel.

SQUARING THE BLADE

Before you begin cutting, it's a good idea to check that your table is square to the blade. Lift the saw arm up to its highest point and place a 2" triangle or a small square beside the blade (see **Figure 5**). If the blade and the square aren't parallel to each other, adjust your table until both the blade and the square line up.

If you don't have a square or triangle, try this method using a piece of scrap wood. First, make a small cut in a piece of scrap wood (see **Figure 6**). Then, turn the scrap wood until the cut is facing the back of the blade. Slide the wood across the table so that the blade fits into the cut. If the blade inserts easily into the cut, it is square. If the blade does not insert easily into the cut, adjust the table until the blade is square.

Figure 6. If you don't have a square, you can use a piece of scrap wood to square the table to the blade. First, make a small cut in the piece of scrap wood. Then, slide the cut toward the blade from the back. If the blade fits into the cut easily, the table is square to the blade.

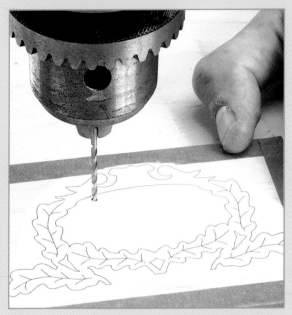

Figure 7. Drill any blade entry holes after adhering the pattern to the wood. Locate the blade entry holes close to the line so that it will take less time for the blade to reach the pattern line.

CREATING AN AUXILIARY TABLE

Most scroll saws on the market today have an opening in the table and around the blade that is much larger than is necesary. This design often causes small and delicate fretwork to break off on the downward stroke of the blade. An easy solution is to add a wooden auxiliary table to the top of the metal table on your saw.

To make an auxiliary table, choose a piece of ¼" to ⅜" plywood that is similar to the size of your current saw's table. If you wish, you can cut this plywood to the same shape as the metal table on your saw, or to any shape or size you prefer. We do recommend, however, that you make the table larger than what you think you will need for the size of the projects you will make in the future.

Next, set the auxiliary table on top of the metal table. From the underside of the metal table, use a pencil to mark the location where the blade will feed through. Then, turn the auxiliary table over and drill a ¹⁄₁₆"- to ⅛"-diameter hole, or a hole slightly larger than the blade you will be using.

Finally, apply a few strips of double-sided carpet tape to the metal table on each side of the blade. Firmly press the auxiliary table onto the double-sided carpet tape, making sure that the blade is centered in the hole.

DRILLING BLADE ENTRY HOLES

If your project requires blade entry holes, be sure to drill all of them once you have adhered the paper pattern to the workpiece with repositionable spray adhesive. When drilling blade entry holes, it is best to drill close to the line, rather than in the middle of the waste areas, because it will take less time for the blade to reach the pattern line (see **Figure 7**). Sand the back of the piece to remove any burrs before you begin cutting.

VEINING

Veining is a simple technique that will bring a lifelike appearance to your project. The veins of a leaf or the folds of clothing will look more realistic when this technique is incorporated.

To vein, simply choose a thin blade (usually smaller than #7) and saw all solid black lines, as indicated on the pattern. You will be able to vein some areas of the pattern by sawing inward from the outside edge; in other areas, you will need to drill a tiny blade entry hole for the blade (see **Figure 8**).

If you wish to make a project easier, simply omit the veining.

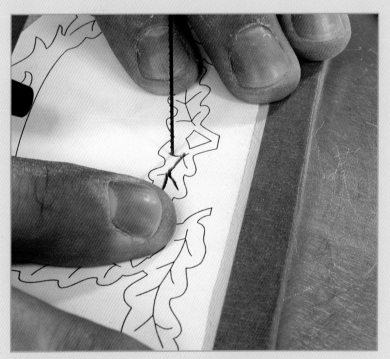

Figure 8. Veining can give your projects a lifelike appearance. The type of veining shown here requires a blade entry hole in order to make the cuts.

STACK CUTTING

Stack cutting is fairly simple to do and can save you a lot of time when you have two or more identical pieces to cut for a project or if you are making more than one of a particular project. If you are fairly new to scroll sawing and stack cutting, we recommend cutting no more than a total thickness of ½" for best results.

On projects with fairly simple shapes, two or three layers could be held together by double-sided tape or by paper sprayed on both sides with repositionable adhesive and sandwiched between the workpieces. You could also put masking tape on each edge of the stack to hold the pattern and the workpieces in place (see **Figure 9**).

On more intricate projects, we suggest using #18 wire nails or brads that are slightly longer than the total thickness of the stack you are cutting. Tack the nails into the waste areas you will cut out, along with a few around the outside of the project. If the nail has gone through the bottom of the workpiece, use a hammer to tap it flush or use coarse sandpaper to sand the points flush with the bottom of the workpiece.

If you are stack cutting hardwoods, do not tack the nail too close to the pattern line or it may cause the wood to split. You could also predrill holes for the nails with a slightly smaller drill bit so the nail will fit snugly and hold the layers together securely.

SAWING THIN WOODS

Thin hardwoods or plywoods can be difficult to work with because they're prone to breaking. The following suggestions should help to eliminate or reduce this problem.

■ If you have a variable speed saw, reduce the speed to ½ to ¾ of high speed.

■ If you do not have a variable speed saw, it will help to stack cut two or more layers of material to prevent breakage.

■ For cutting any thickness of material, it is very beneficial to keep the fingers of at least one hand, if not both, partially touching the table for better control (see **Figure 10**).

■ With any material, it is important that your feed rate and blade speed match so that burn marks won't appear on the wood. If you prefer to feed the wood into the blade slowly, set your saw on a slow setting or try using a smaller blade with more teeth per inch to slow down the speed at which the blade is cutting. On the other hand, if you prefer to feed the wood into the blade quickly, choose a fast setting for your saw or try using a blade with fewer teeth per inch.

Figure 9. Masking tape or painter's tape (shown) placed around the edges can be used to hold a stack together. Some scrollers also like to cover the surface of the wood with tape before adhering the pattern to help lubricate the blade as it cuts. Double-sided tape placed in the corners of the workpieces can also be an effective method of holding the stack together.

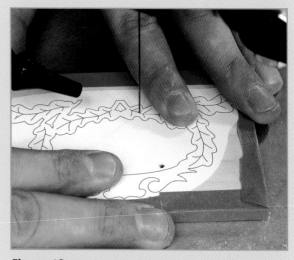

Figure 10. Keeping some of the fingers of both hands in contact with the surface can give you better control.

FINISHING TECHNIQUES

The finishing of the plate projects can be done before or after assembling. For many of the pieces, especially those with a fair amount of fretwork, it is easier to apply the finish prior to assembling. If you finish the piece before assembling, you also have more options for using contrasting stains.

If you've made your project from hardwood, we recommend dipping it in a dishpan (or a similar container) filled with a penetrating oil, such as Watco or tung (see **Figure 11**). After dipping the project, allow the excess oil to drain back into the pan, and then follow the manufacturer's instructions.

If you have chosen to use plywood, such as Baltic birch, we recommend using two slightly different shades of stain in order to give an appealing contrast to the finished project.

As a final finish step, use a clear, Varathane-type spray for a protective coating.

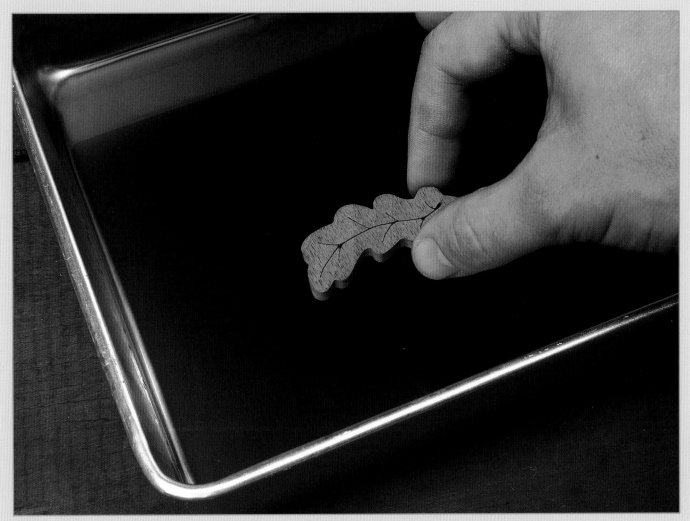

Figure 11. If you have used hardwood for your project, an easy method of finishing is to dip it in a dishpan or a similar container filled with a penetrating oil.

Figure 12. After applying glue to the tabs of the interior design, align the rim and press the design into place. Then, attach any overlays.

ASSEMBLY

Assembly of the plate is very simple. First, apply a small amount of glue or silicone to each tab of the interior design. Then, align the rim over the tabs and press it into position (see **Figure 12**). Use glue or silicone to attach any overlays.

CUSTOMIZING YOUR PROJECT

There are several options available to help you customize your collector plate project. If you have chosen plywood for parts of your project, veneers are an excellent way to add contrast. When gluing veneers to your workpieces, it is important to glue the veneer to both sides of your material. This will help to prevent the plywood from warping or cupping.

If the wall where you prefer to display your plates does not provide enough contrast for the design to stand out as well as you would like, add a contrasting backing behind the plate, such as colored paper or material. Another option is to use overlays to dress up and customize a plain rim. These can be found on page 122.

Many of the rims and interior designs in this book are designed to be interchangeable with each other. This will allow you to be creative and to customize your own collectible plate masterpiece. You may need to enlarge or reduce the interior design to fit the rim, or even to eliminate or reposition the tabs.

You can also enlarge or reduce the size of the projects. Try making one project at full-size and then a few projects at 50% to 75% for a striking display. Remember to enlarge or reduce all of the pieces by the same percentages. You'll also want to change the thickness of your material in relation to the enlargement or reduction of the piece. For example, if you make a piece that is twice as large, you'll need material that is twice as thick.

Deer Duo, pattern on page 18.

Meadow Elegance, pattern on page 26.

Where the Buffalo Roam, pattern on page 30.

Majesty, pattern on page 46.

Taking Aim, pattern on page 54.

Friend of the Flowers, pattern on page 66.

Making a Splash, pattern on page 100.

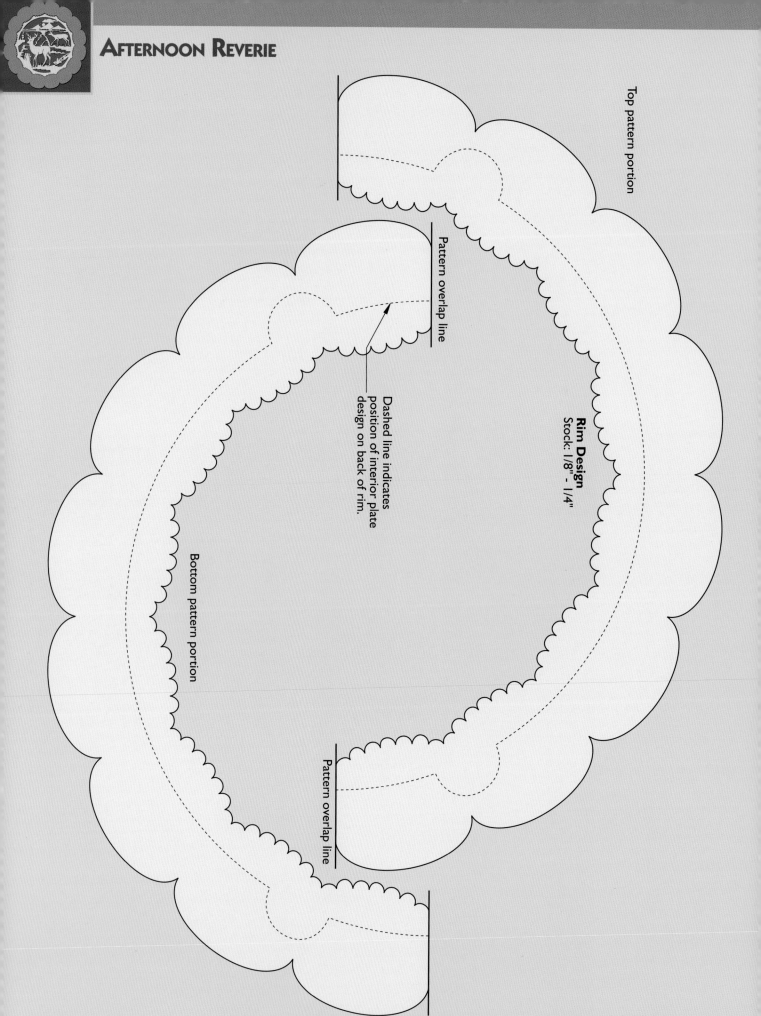

Top pattern portion

Pattern overlap line

Dashed line indicates
position of interior plate
design on back of rim.

Rim Design
Stock: 1/8" - 1/4"

Bottom pattern portion

Pattern overlap line

Interior Plate Design
Stock: 1/4" - 3/8"

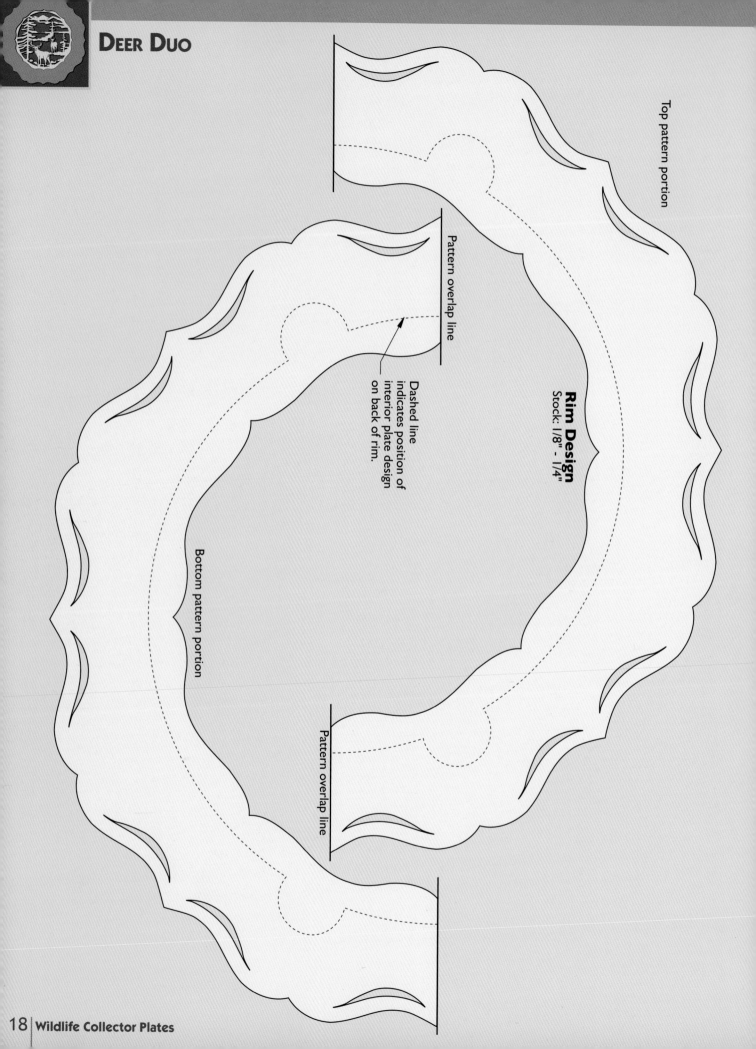

DEER DUO

Top pattern portion

Pattern overlap line

Rim Design
Stock: 1/8" - 1/4"

Dashed line
indicates position of
interior plate design
on back of rim.

Bottom pattern portion

Pattern overlap line

Interior Plate Design
Stock: 1/4" - 3/8"

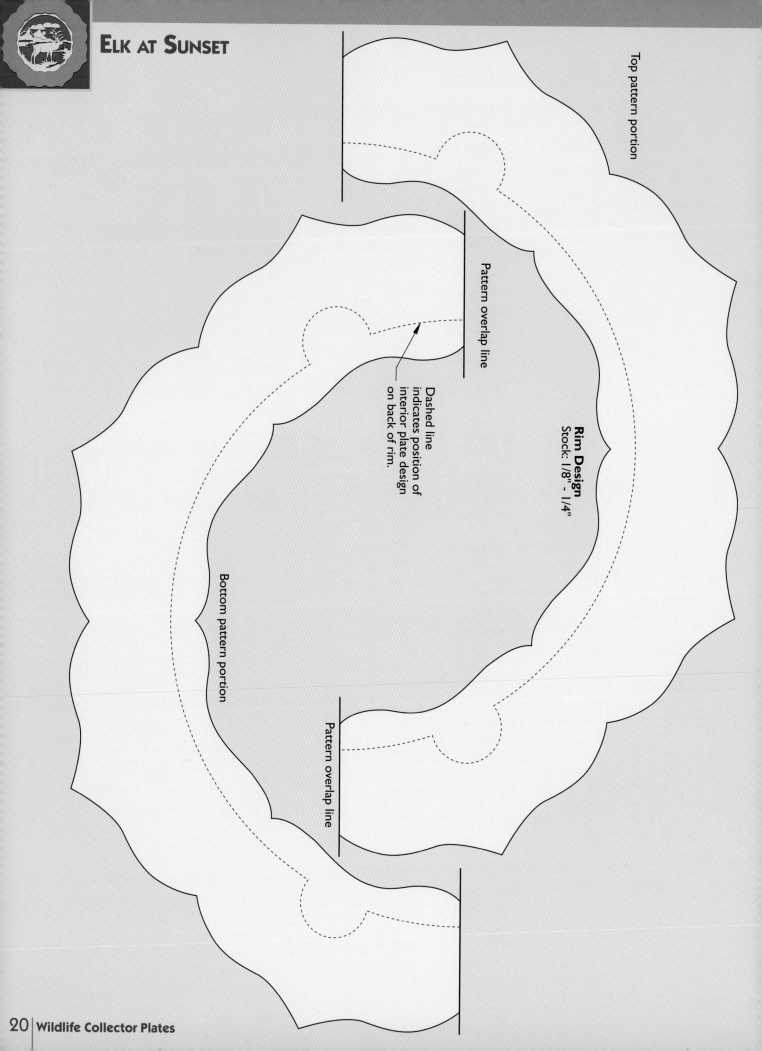

ELK AT SUNSET

Top pattern portion

Pattern overlap line

Rim Design
Stock: 1/8" - 1/4"

Dashed line
indicates position of
interior plate design
on back of rim.

Bottom pattern portion

Pattern overlap line

Interior Plate Design
Stock: 1/4" - 3/8"

LEAPING STAG

Top Overlay
Stock: 1/16" - 1/4"

Rim Design
Stock: 1/8" - 1/4"

Top pattern portion

Pattern overlap line

Small dashed line indicates
suggested position of leaf overlay.

Small dashed line
indicates position of
top overlay.

Dashed line indicates
position of interior plate
design behind rim.

Pattern overlap line

Bottom pattern portion

Small dashed line
indicates position of
bottom overlay.

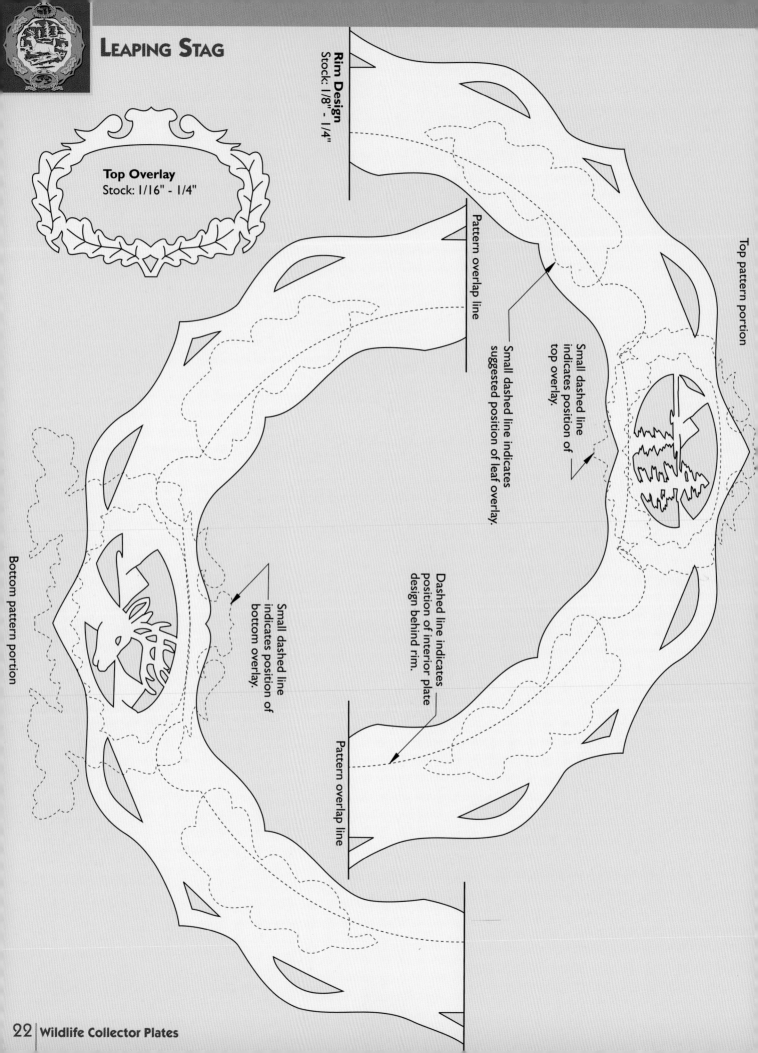

Interior Plate Design
Stock: 1/4" - 3/8"

Leaf Overlay
Stock: 1/16" - 1/4"

Bottom Overlay
Stock: 1/16" - 1/4"

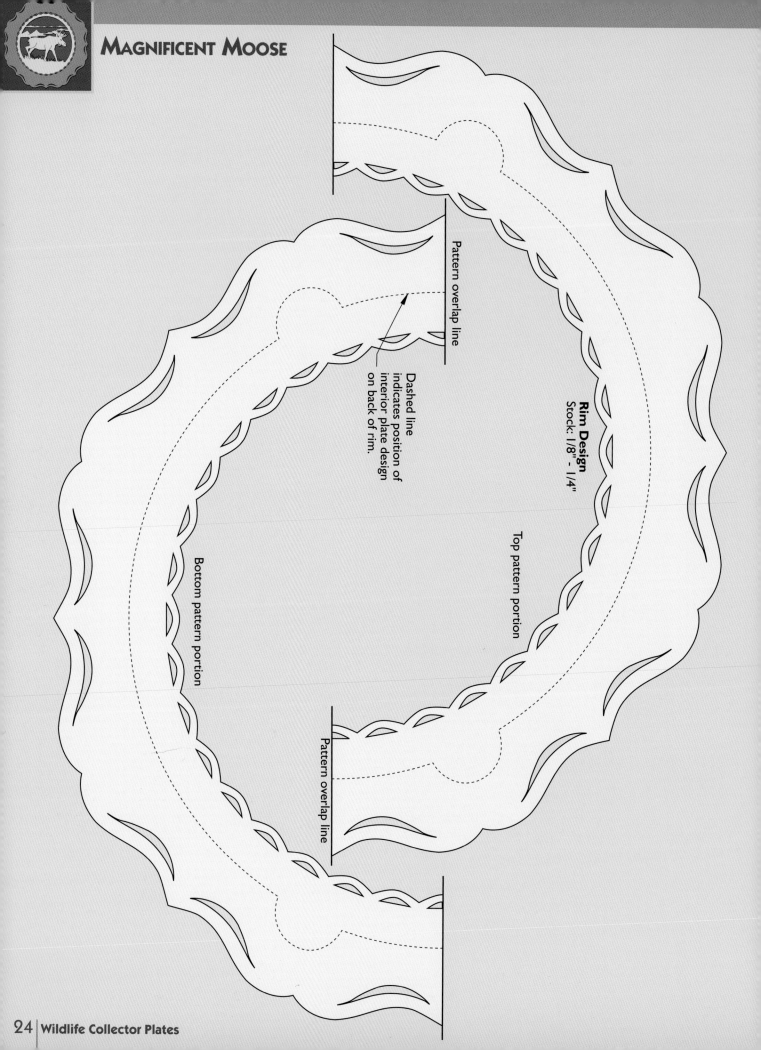

Rim Design
Stock: 1/8" - 1/4"

Pattern overlap line

Dashed line
indicates position of
interior plate design
on back of rim.

Top pattern portion

Bottom pattern portion

Pattern overlap line

Interior Plate Design
Stock: 1/4" - 3/8"

MEADOW ELEGANCE

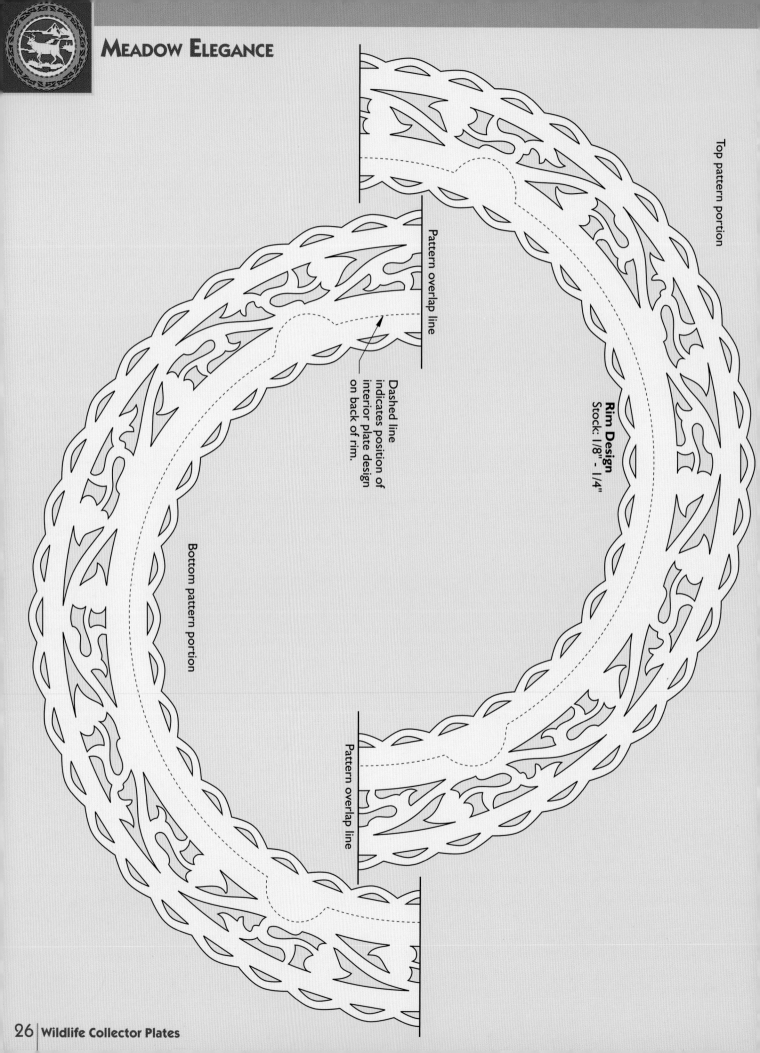

Top pattern portion

Rim Design
Stock: 1/8" - 1/4"

Pattern overlap line

Dashed line
indicates position of
interior plate design
on back of rim.

Bottom pattern portion

Pattern overlap line

Interior Plate Design
Stock: 1/4" - 3/8"

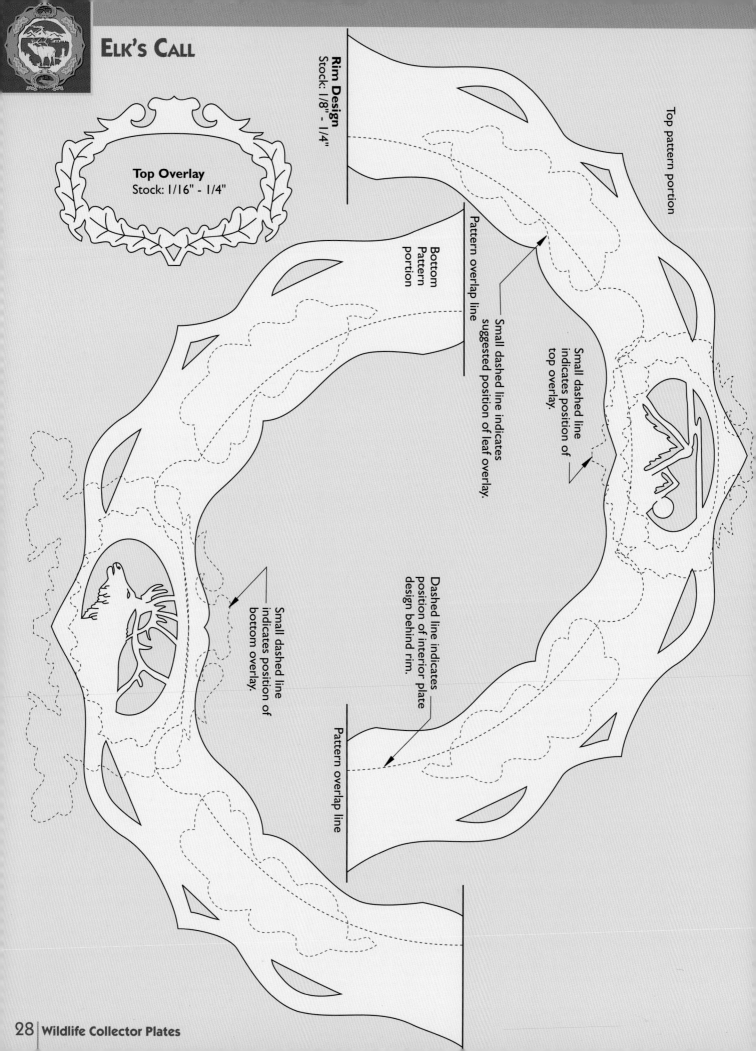

ELK'S CALL

Top Overlay
Stock: 1/16" - 1/4"

Rim Design
Stock: 1/8" - 1/4"

Top pattern portion

Bottom Pattern portion

Pattern overlap line

Small dashed line indicates suggested position of leaf overlay.

Small dashed line indicates position of top overlay.

Dashed line indicates position of interior plate design behind rim.

Pattern overlap line

Small dashed line indicates position of bottom overlay.

ELK'S CALL

Interior Plate Design
Stock: 1/4" - 3/8"

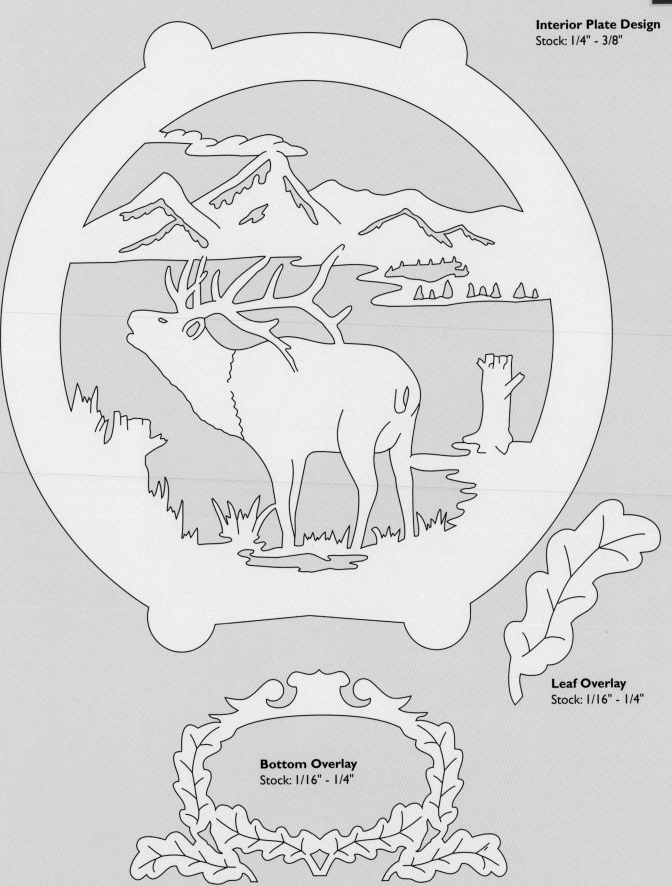

Leaf Overlay
Stock: 1/16" - 1/4"

Bottom Overlay
Stock: 1/16" - 1/4"

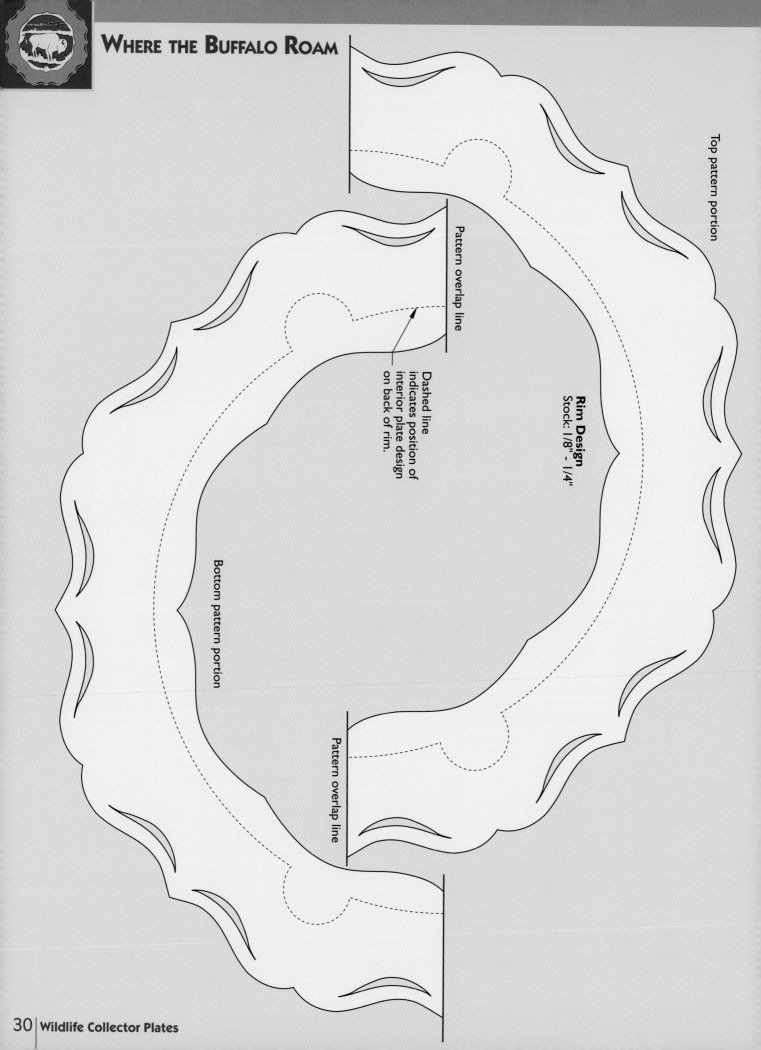

Top pattern portion

Pattern overlap line

Dashed line
indicates position of
interior plate design
on back of rim.

Rim Design
Stock: 1/8" - 1/4"

Bottom pattern portion

Pattern overlap line

Interior Plate Design
Stock: 1/4" - 3/8"

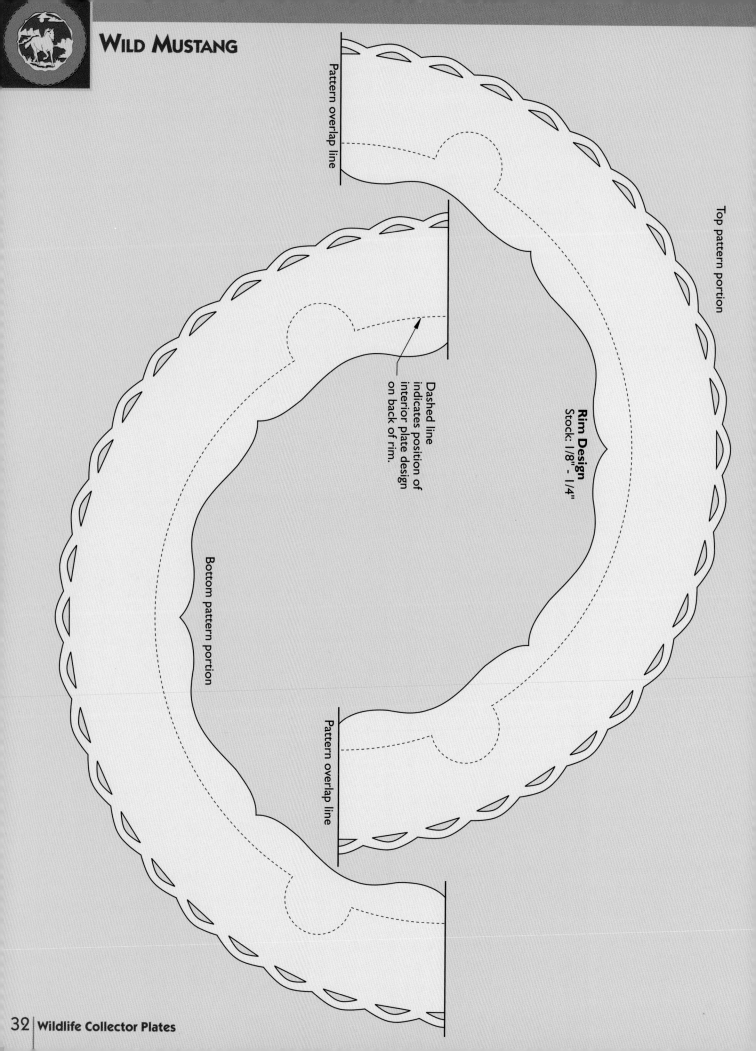

Pattern overlap line

Top pattern portion

Rim Design
Stock: 1/8" - 1/4"

Dashed line
indicates position of
interior plate design
on back of rim.

Bottom pattern portion

Pattern overlap line

Interior Plate Design
Stock: 1/4" - 3/8"

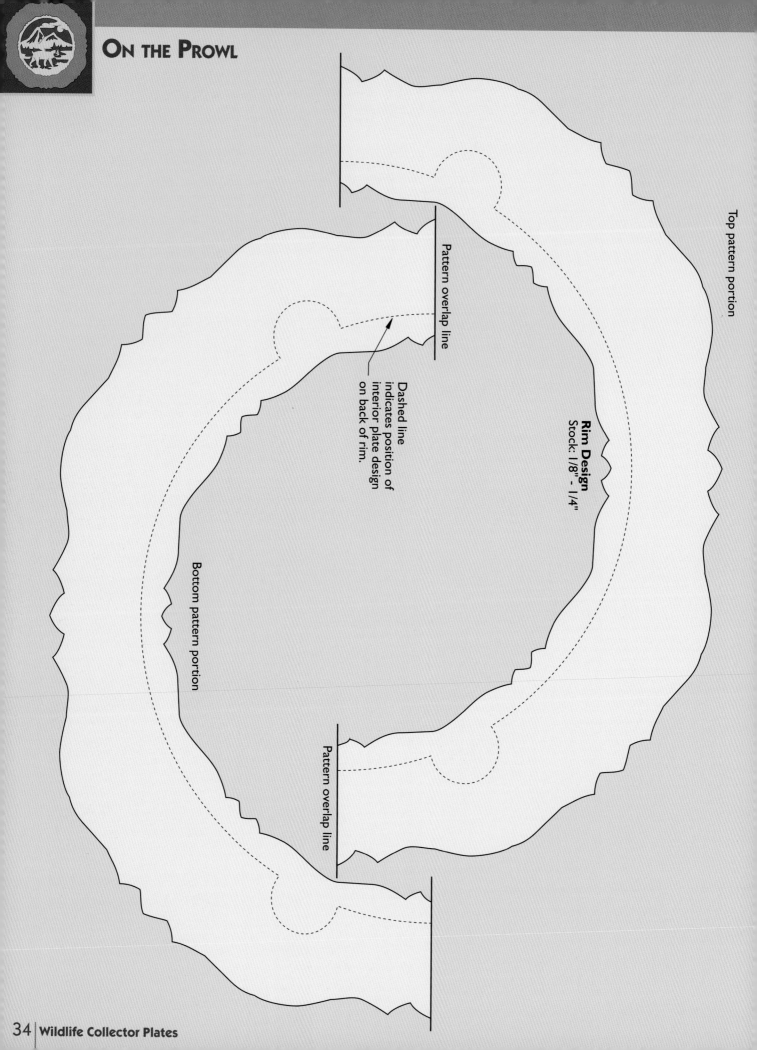

Top pattern portion

Pattern overlap line

Rim Design
Stock: 1/8" - 1/4"

Dashed line indicates position of interior plate design on back of rim.

Bottom pattern portion

Pattern overlap line

Pattern overlap line

Interior Plate Design
Stock: 1/4" – 3/8"

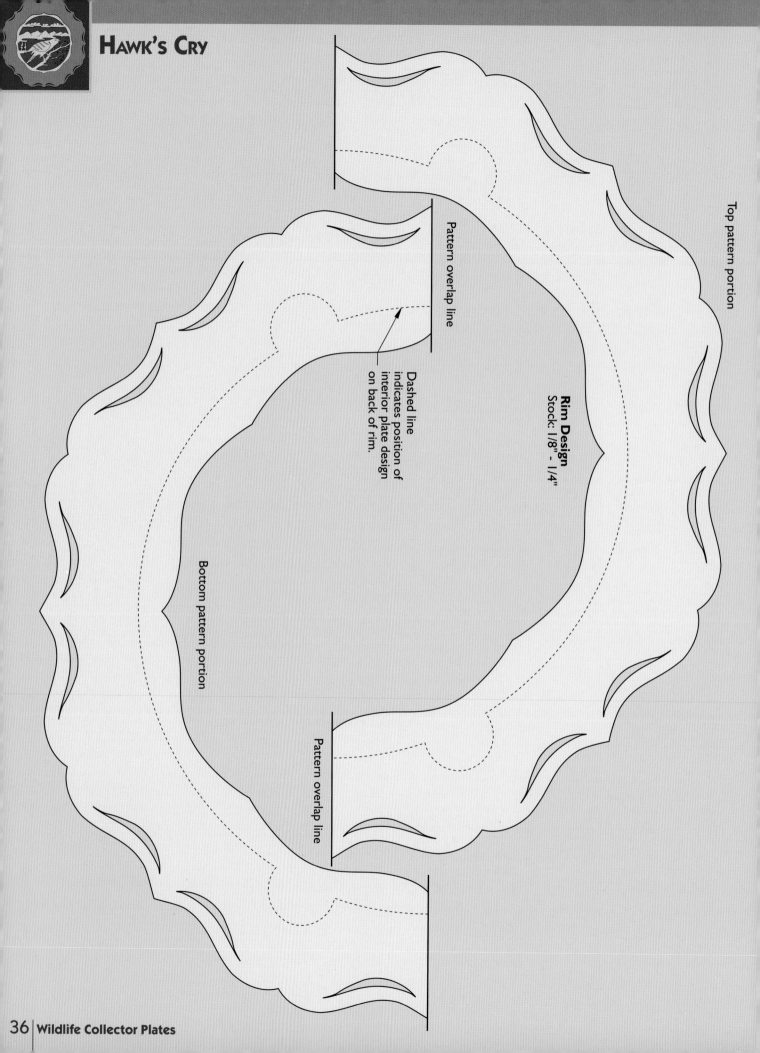

Top pattern portion

Pattern overlap line

Rim Design
Stock: 1/8" - 1/4"

Dashed line
indicates position of
interior plate design
on back of rim.

Bottom pattern portion

Pattern overlap line

Interior Plate Design
Stock: 1/4" - 3/8"

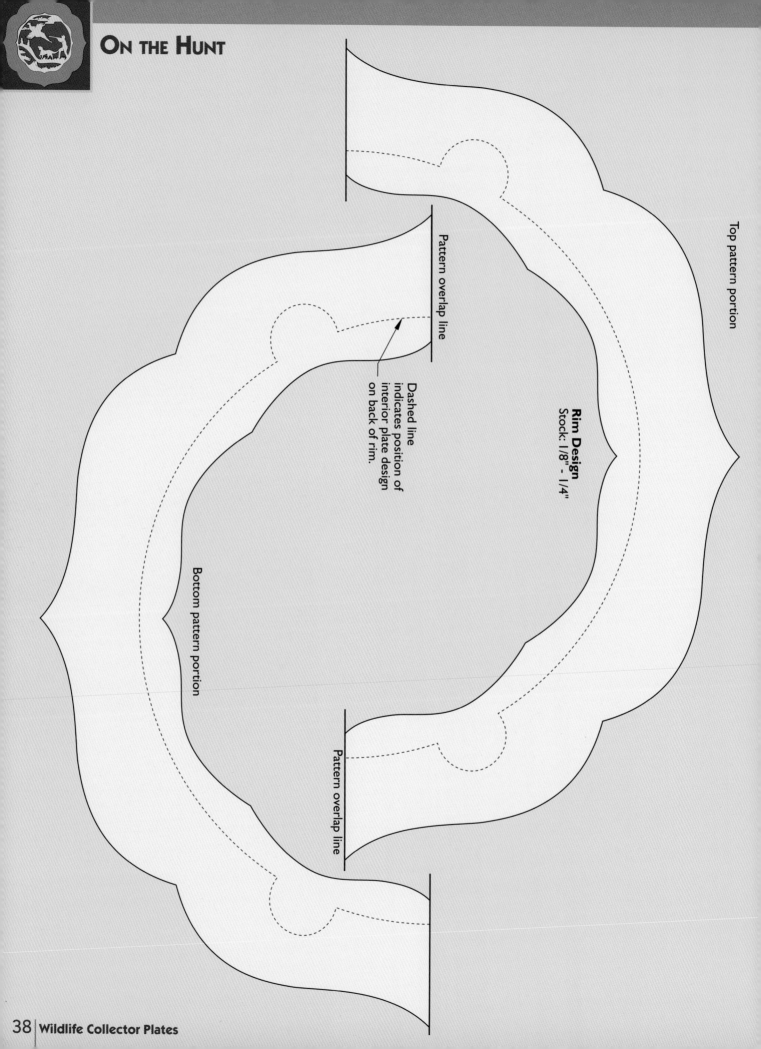

Top pattern portion

Rim Design
Stock: 1/8" - 1/4"

Pattern overlap line

Dashed line
indicates position of
interior plate design
on back of rim.

Bottom pattern portion

Pattern overlap line

Interior Plate Design
Stock: 1/4" - 3/8"

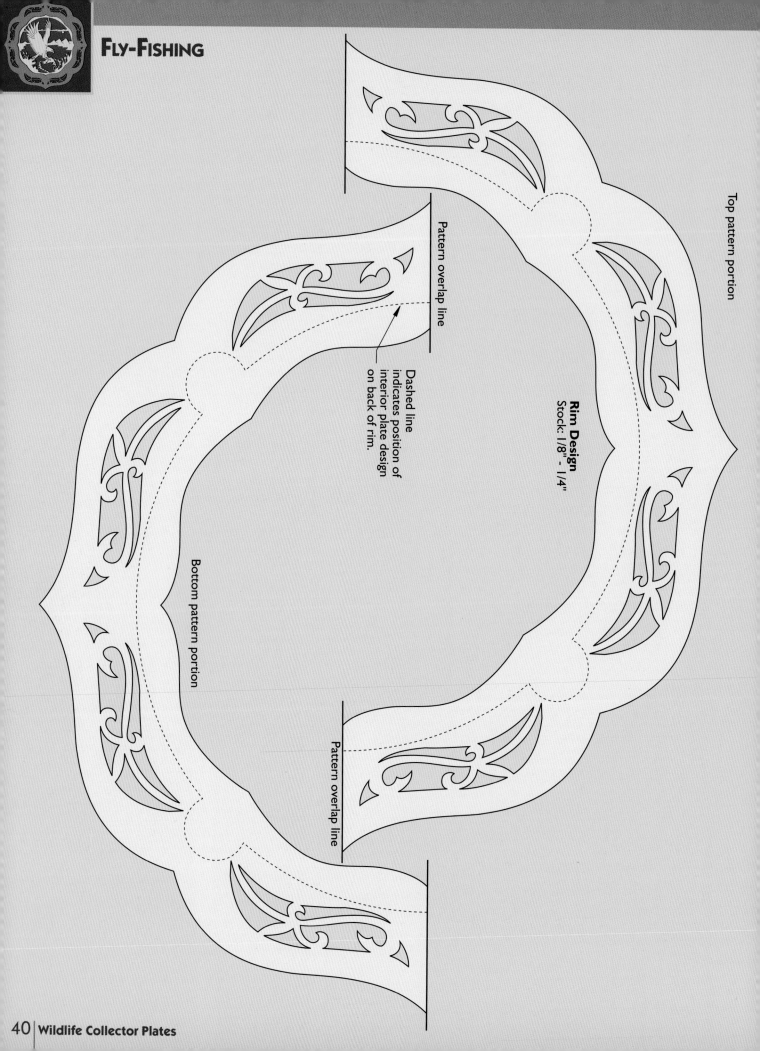

Top pattern portion

Rim Design
Stock: 1/8" - 1/4"

Pattern overlap line

Dashed line
indicates position of
interior plate design
on back of rim.

Bottom pattern portion

Pattern overlap line

Interior Plate Design
Stock: 1/4" - 3/8"

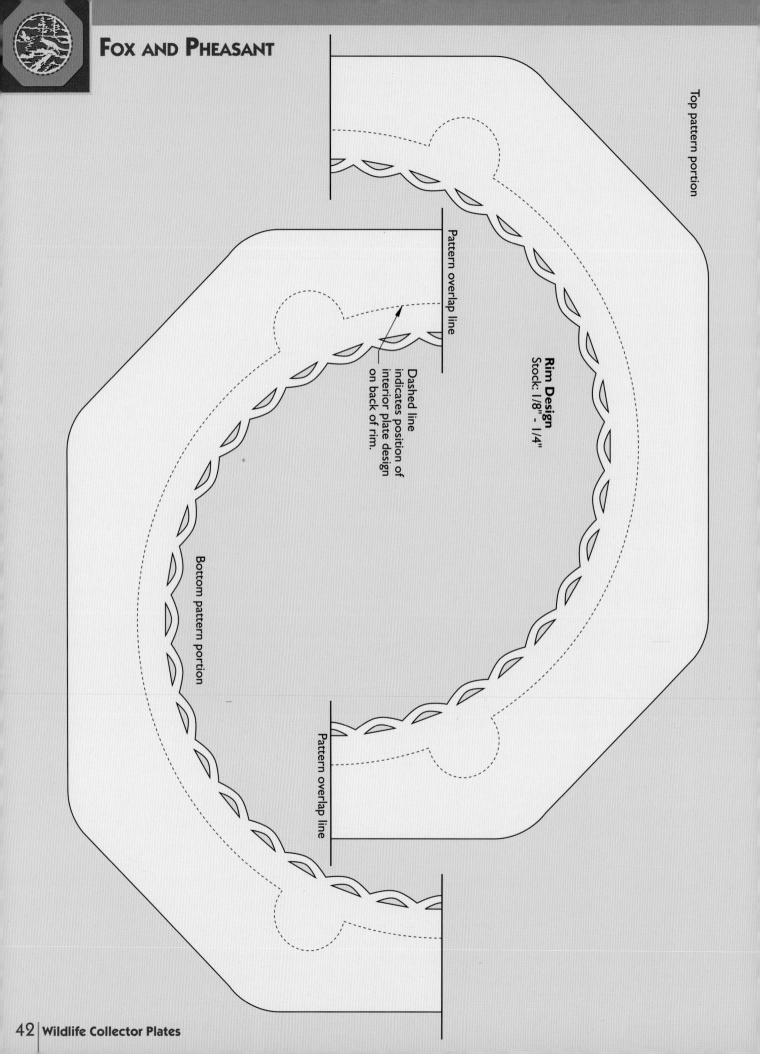

Top pattern portion

Pattern overlap line

Rim Design
Stock: 1/8" - 1/4"

Dashed line
indicates position of
interior plate design
on back of rim.

Bottom pattern portion

Pattern overlap line

Interior Plate Design
Stock: 1/4" - 3/8"

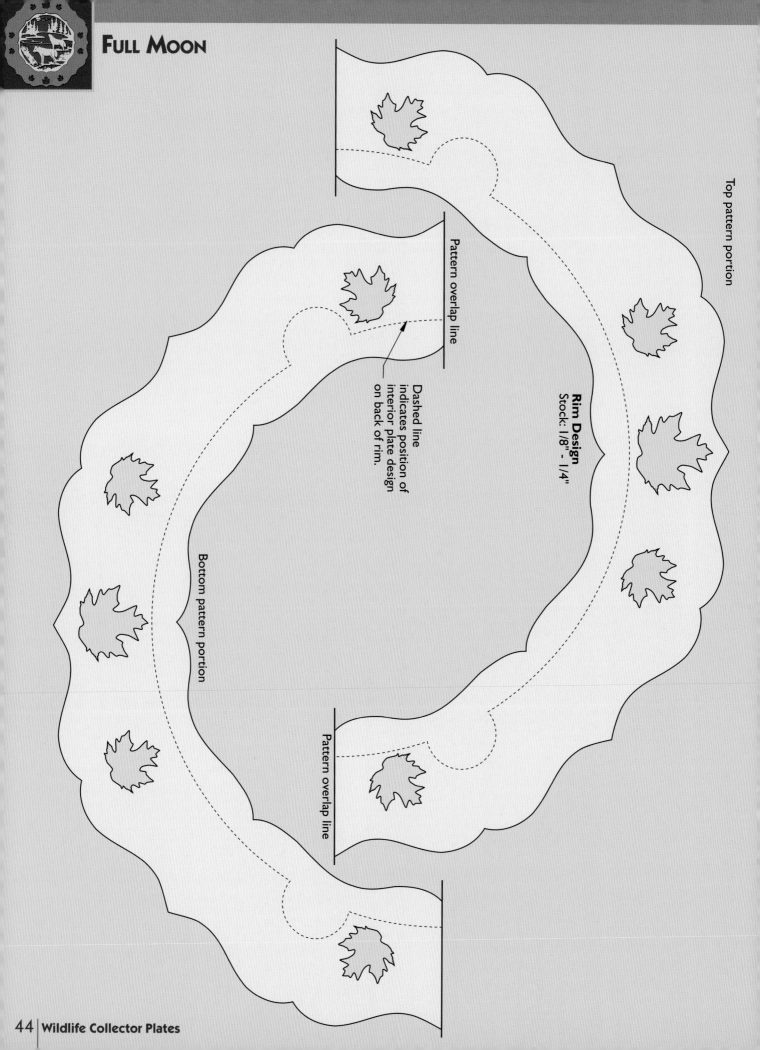

Top pattern portion

Rim Design
Stock: 1/8" – 1/4"

Pattern overlap line

Dashed line
indicates position of
interior plate design
on back of rim.

Bottom pattern portion

Pattern overlap line

Interior Plate Design
Stock: 1/4" - 3/8"

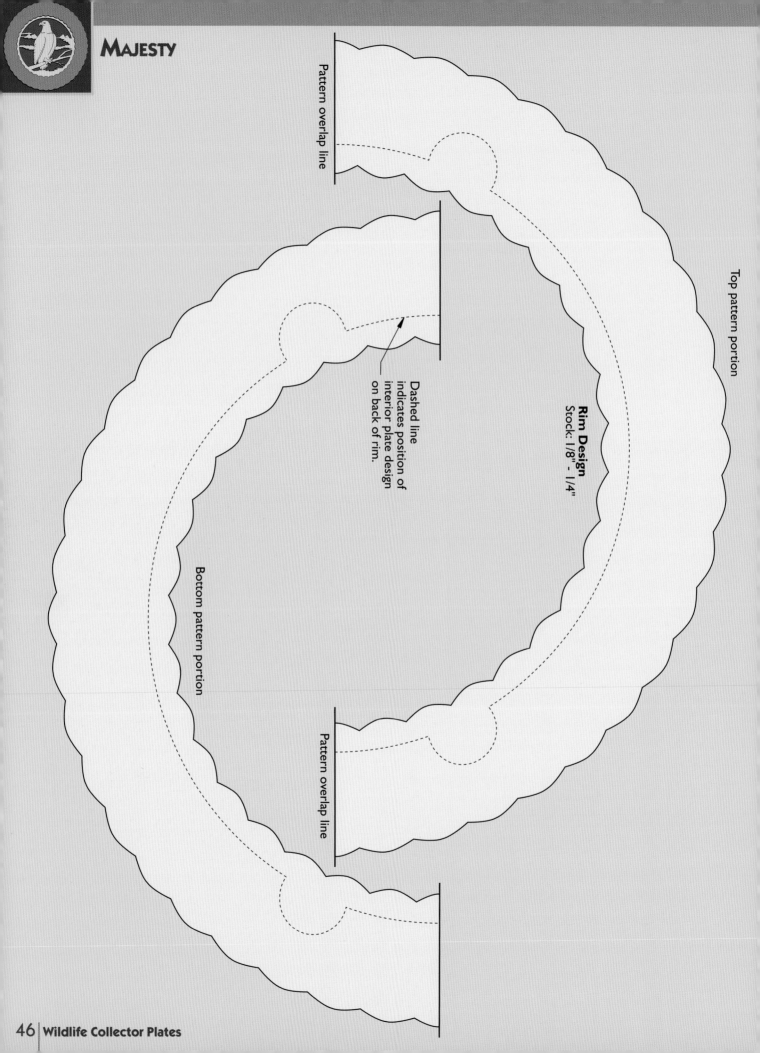

Pattern overlap line

Top pattern portion

Rim Design
Stock: 1/8" – 1/4"

Dashed line
indicates position of
interior plate design
on back of rim.

Bottom pattern portion

Pattern overlap line

Interior Plate Design
Stock: 1/4" - 3/8"

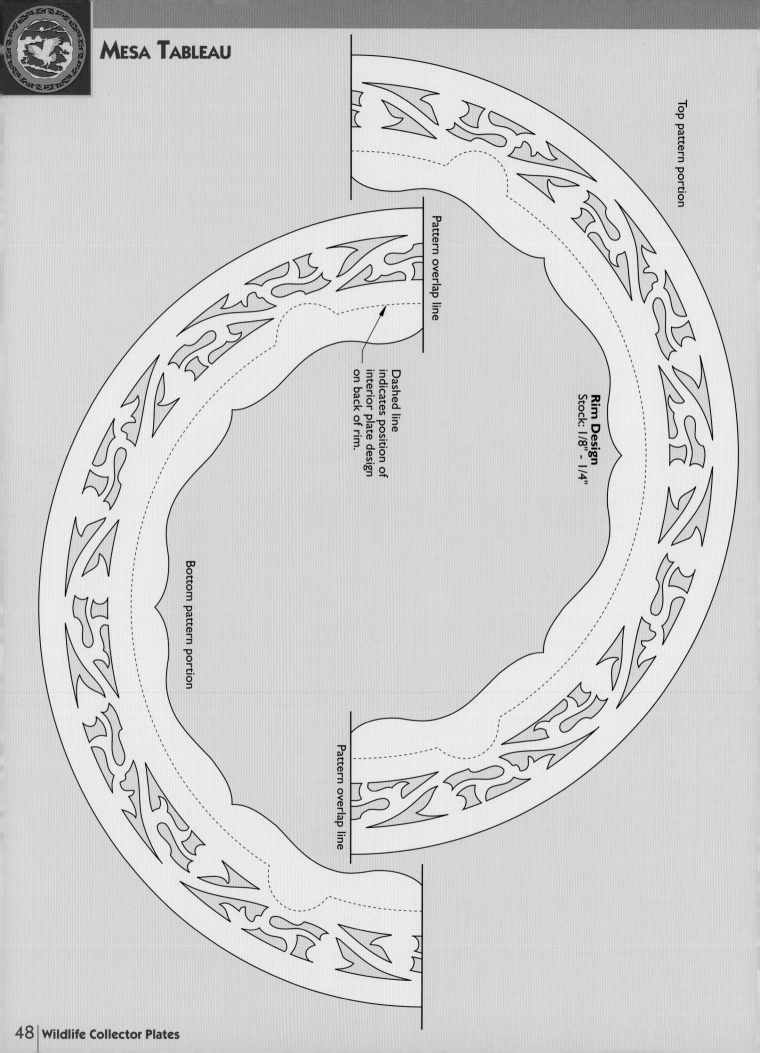

Top pattern portion

Pattern overlap line

Dashed line
indicates position of
interior plate design
on back of rim.

Rim Design
Stock: 1/8" – 1/4"

Bottom pattern portion

Pattern overlap line

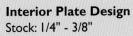

Interior Plate Design
Stock: 1/4" - 3/8"

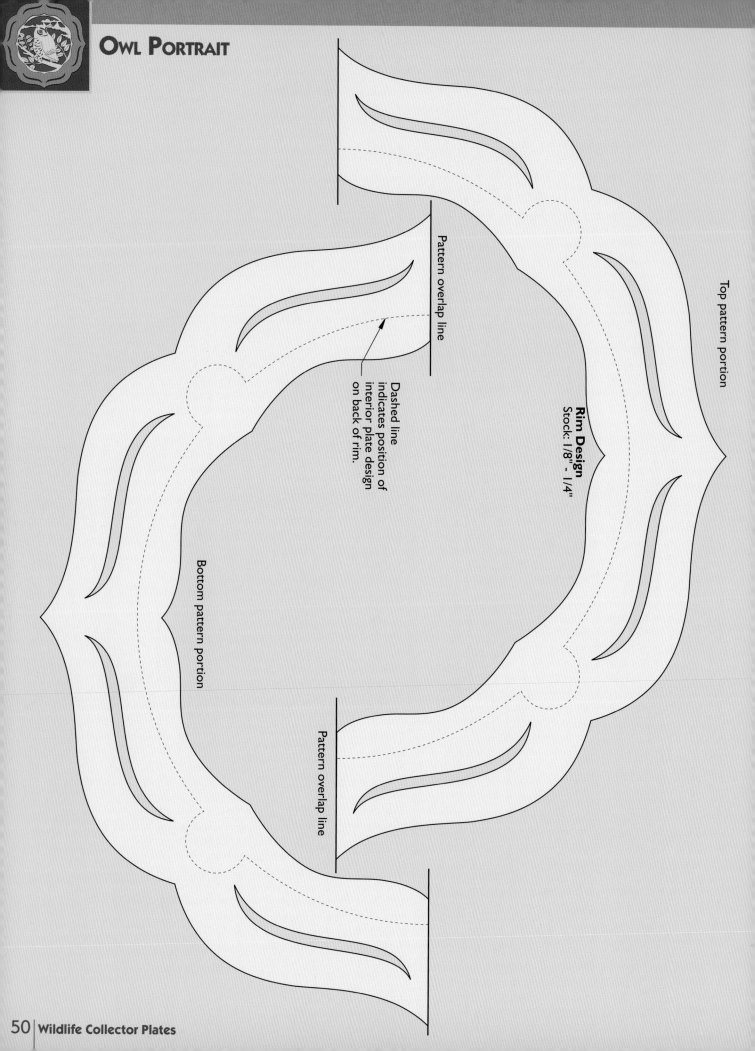

Top pattern portion

Pattern overlap line

Rim Design
Stock: 1/8" - 1/4"

Dashed line
indicates position of
interior plate design
on back of rim.

Bottom pattern portion

Pattern overlap line

Interior Plate Design
Stock: 1/4" - 3/8"

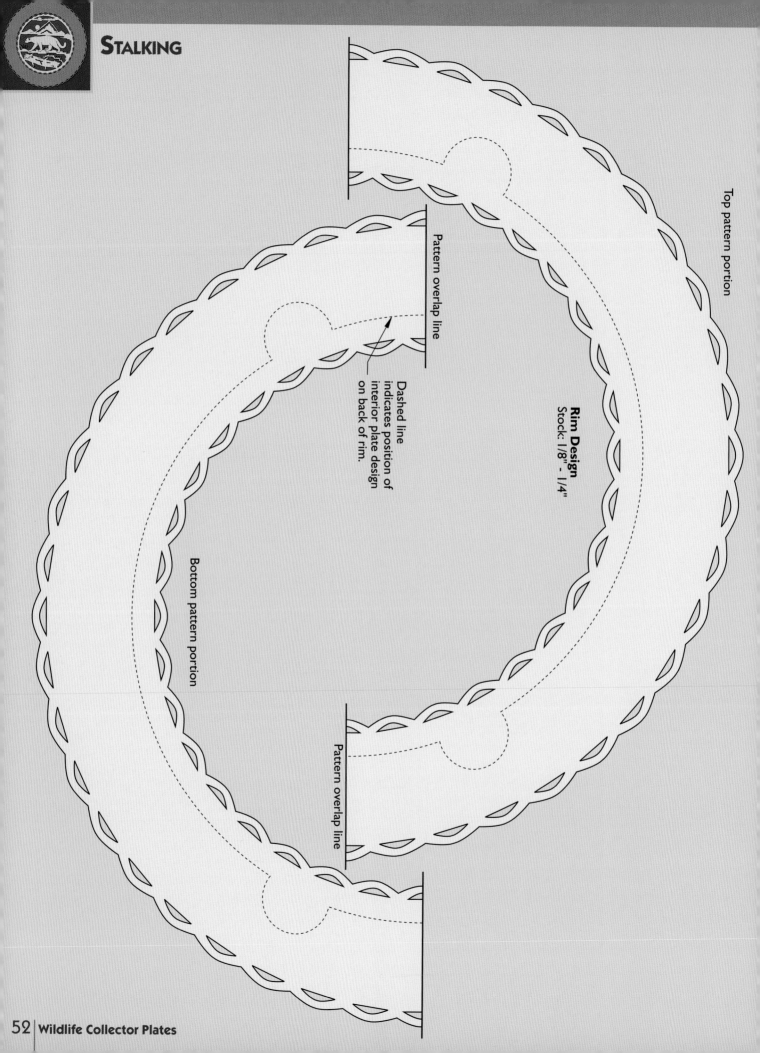

Top pattern portion

Rim Design
Stock: 1/8" - 1/4"

Pattern overlap line

Dashed line
indicates position of
interior plate design
on back of rim.

Pattern overlap line

Bottom pattern portion

Pattern overlap line

Interior Plate Design
Stock: 1/4" - 3/8"

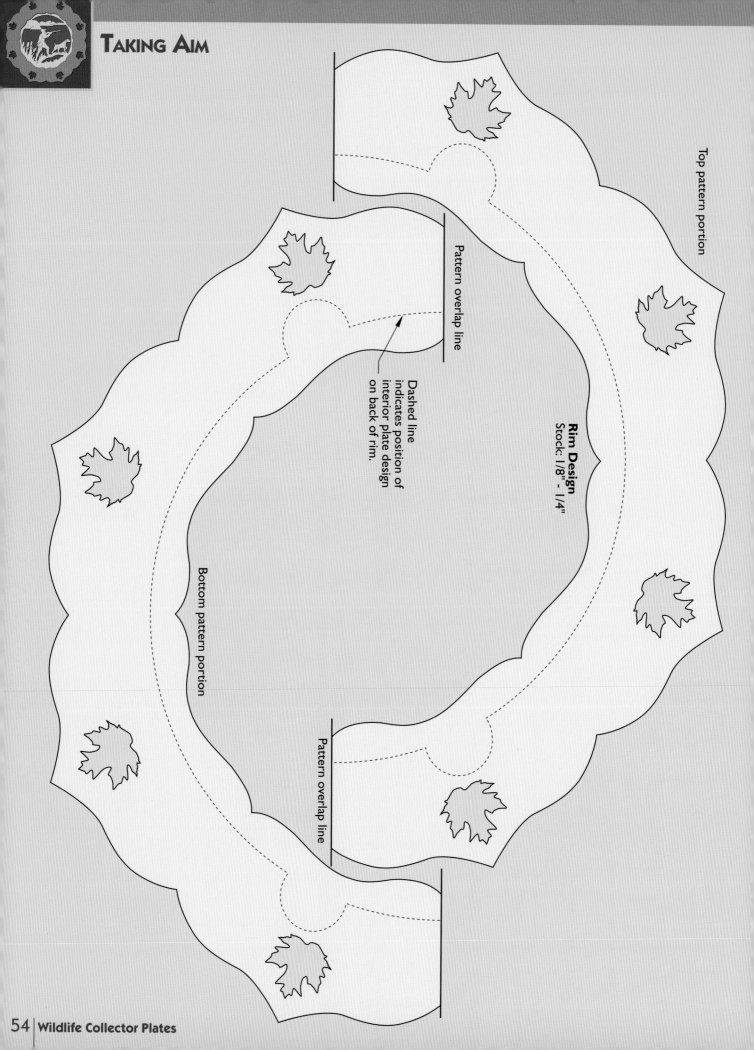

Top pattern portion

Pattern overlap line

Dashed line
indicates position of
interior plate design
on back of rim.

Rim Design
Stock: 1/8" - 1/4"

Bottom pattern portion

Pattern overlap line

Interior Plate Design
Stock: 1/4" - 3/8"

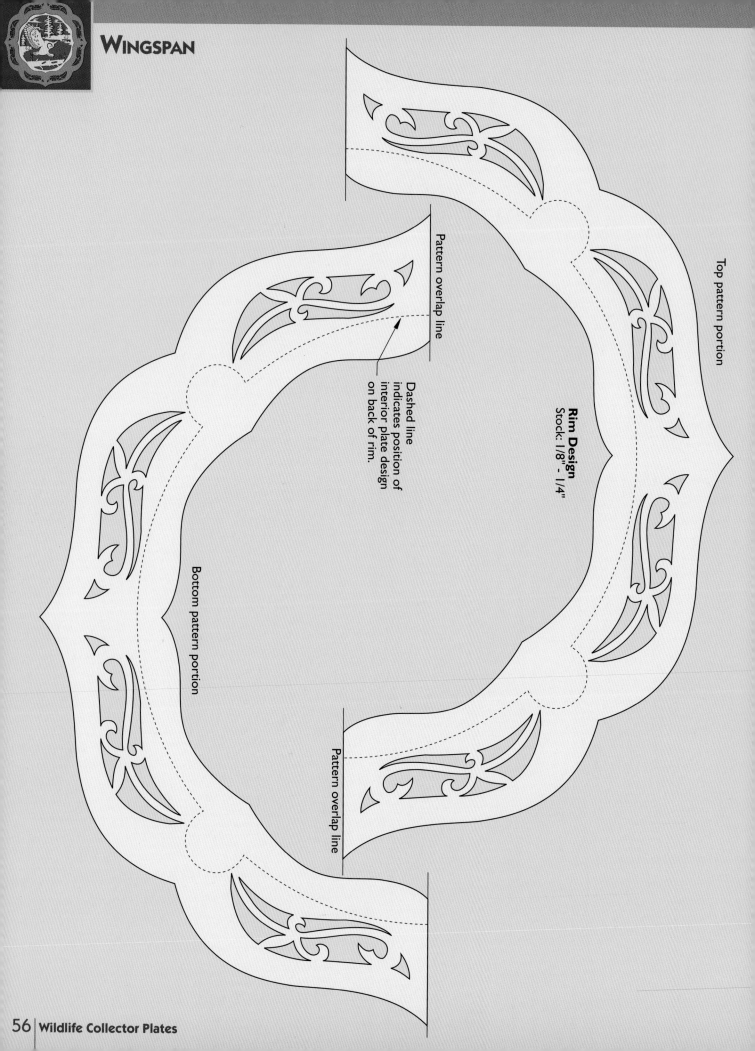

Top pattern portion

Rim Design
Stock: 1/8" - 1/4"

Pattern overlap line

Dashed line indicates position of interior plate design on back of rim.

Bottom pattern portion

Pattern overlap line

Interior Plate Design
Stock: 1/4" - 3/8"

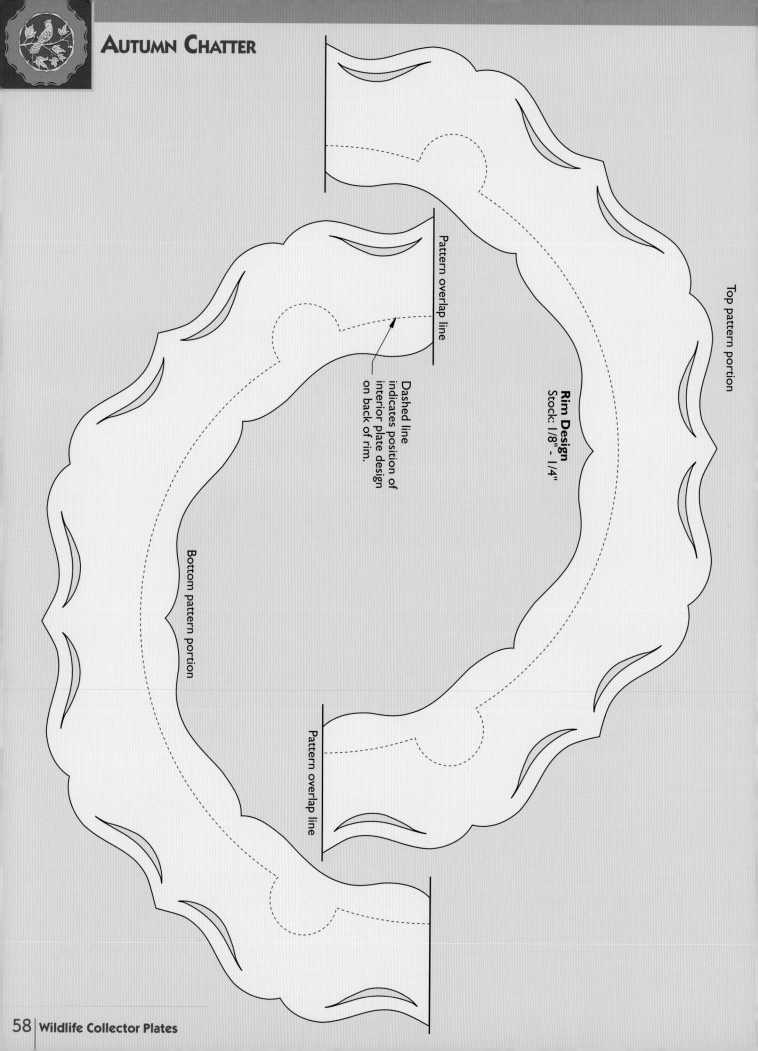

Top pattern portion

Rim Design
Stock: 1/8" - 1/4"

Pattern overlap line

Dashed line
indicates position of
interior plate design
on back of rim.

Bottom pattern portion

Pattern overlap line

Interior Plate Design
Stock: 1/4" - 3/8"

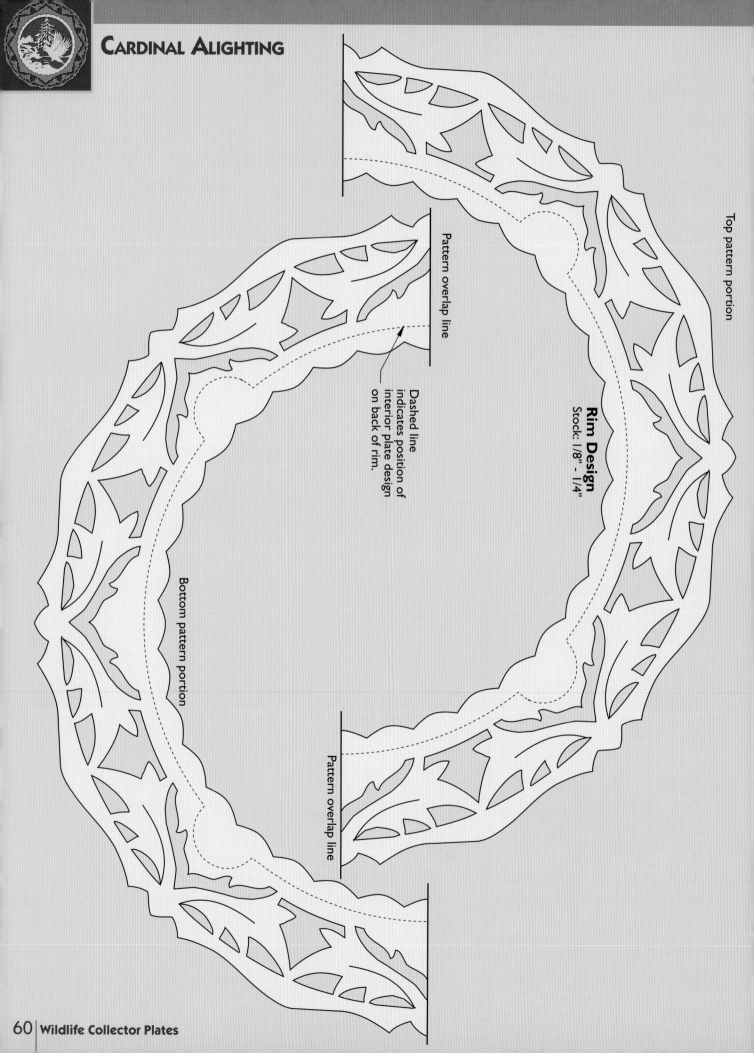

Rim Design
Stock: 1/8" - 1/4"

Top pattern portion

Pattern overlap line

Dashed line indicates position of interior plate design on back of rim.

Pattern overlap line

Bottom pattern portion

Pattern overlap line

Interior Plate Design
Stock: 1/4" - 3/8"

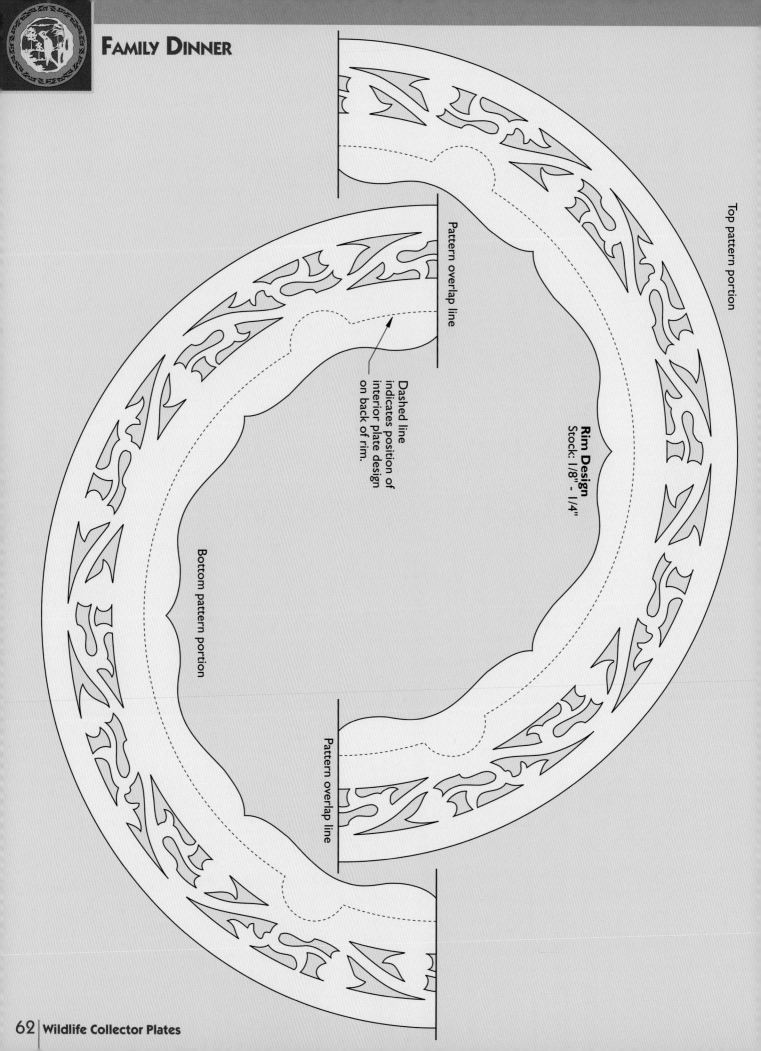

Top pattern portion

Pattern overlap line

Rim Design
Stock: 1/8" - 1/4"

Dashed line indicates position of interior plate design on back of rim.

Bottom pattern portion

Pattern overlap line

Interior Plate Design
Stock: 1/4" - 3/8"

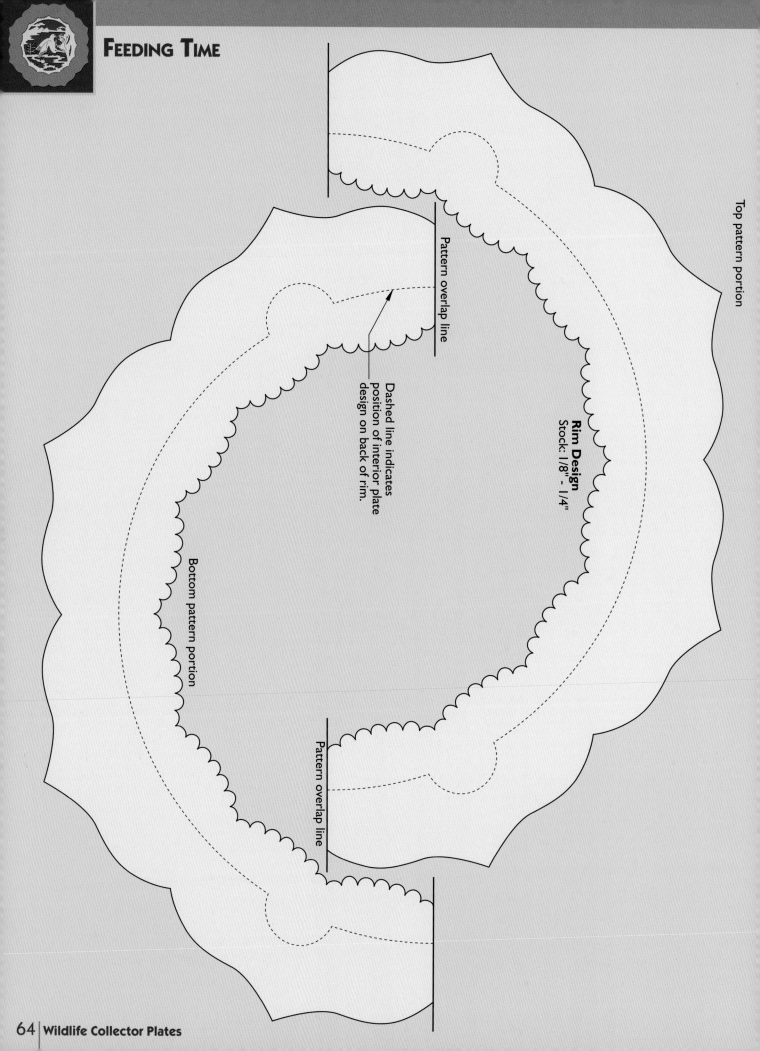

Top pattern portion

Pattern overlap line

Rim Design
Stock: 1/8" - 1/4"

Dashed line indicates
position of interior plate
design on back of rim.

Bottom pattern portion

Pattern overlap line

Pattern overlap line

Interior Plate Design
Stock: 1/4" - 3/8"

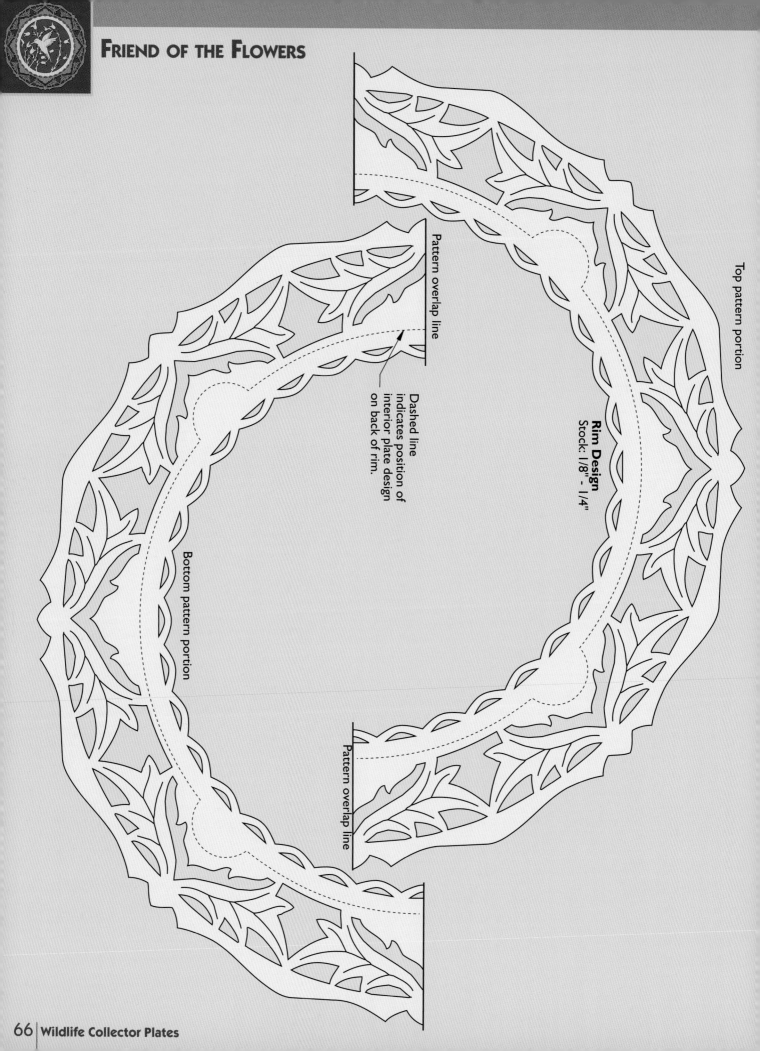

Top pattern portion

Rim Design
Stock: 1/8" - 1/4"

Pattern overlap line

Dashed line
indicates position of
interior plate design
on back of rim.

Bottom pattern portion

Pattern overlap line

Interior Plate Design
Stock: 1/4" - 3/8"

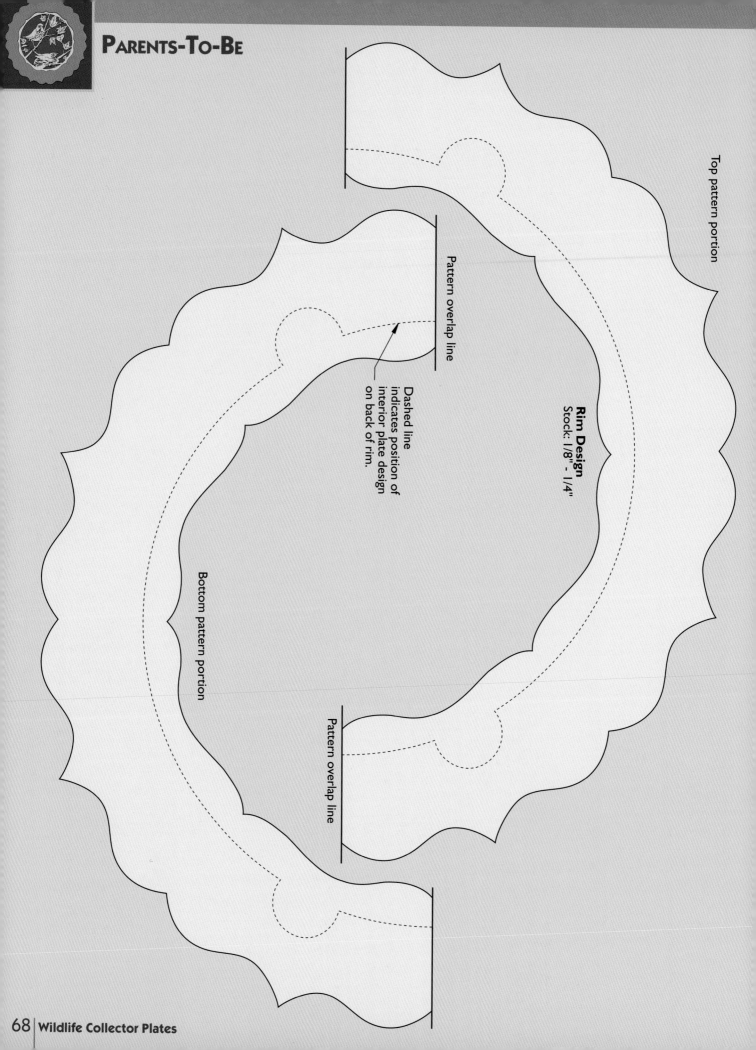

Top pattern portion

Pattern overlap line

Rim Design
Stock: 1/8" - 1/4"

Dashed line
indicates position of
interior plate design
on back of rim.

Bottom pattern portion

Pattern overlap line

Interior Plate Design
Stock: 1/4" - 3/8"

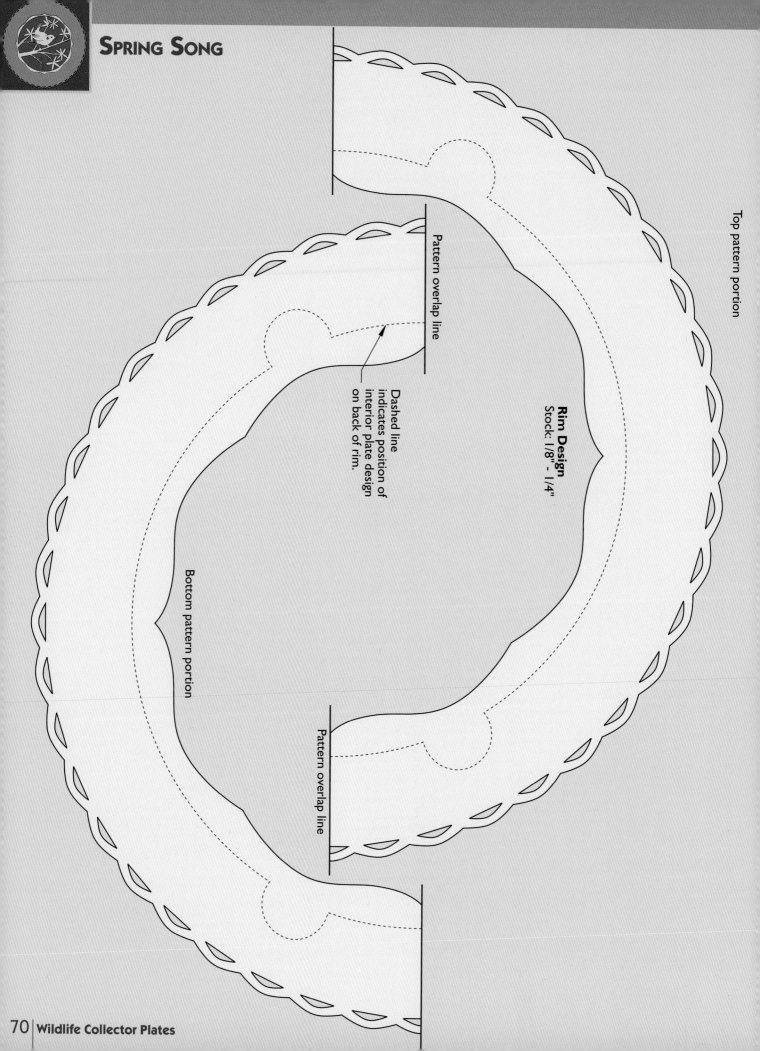

Top pattern portion

Pattern overlap line

Rim Design
Stock: 1/8" - 1/4"

Dashed line
indicates position of
interior plate design
on back of rim.

Bottom pattern portion

Pattern overlap line

Interior Plate Design
Stock: 1/4" - 3/8"

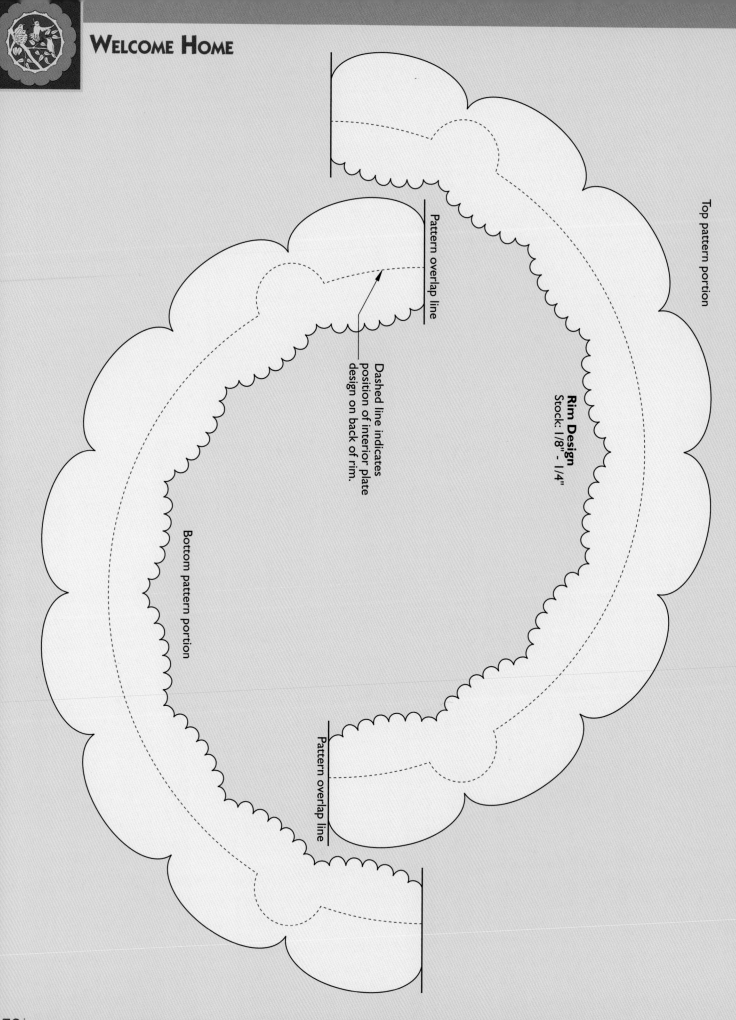

Top pattern portion

Rim Design
Stock: 1/8" - 1/4"

Pattern overlap line

Dashed line indicates
position of interior plate
design on back of rim.

Bottom pattern portion

Pattern overlap line

Interior Plate Design
Stock: 1/4" - 3/8"

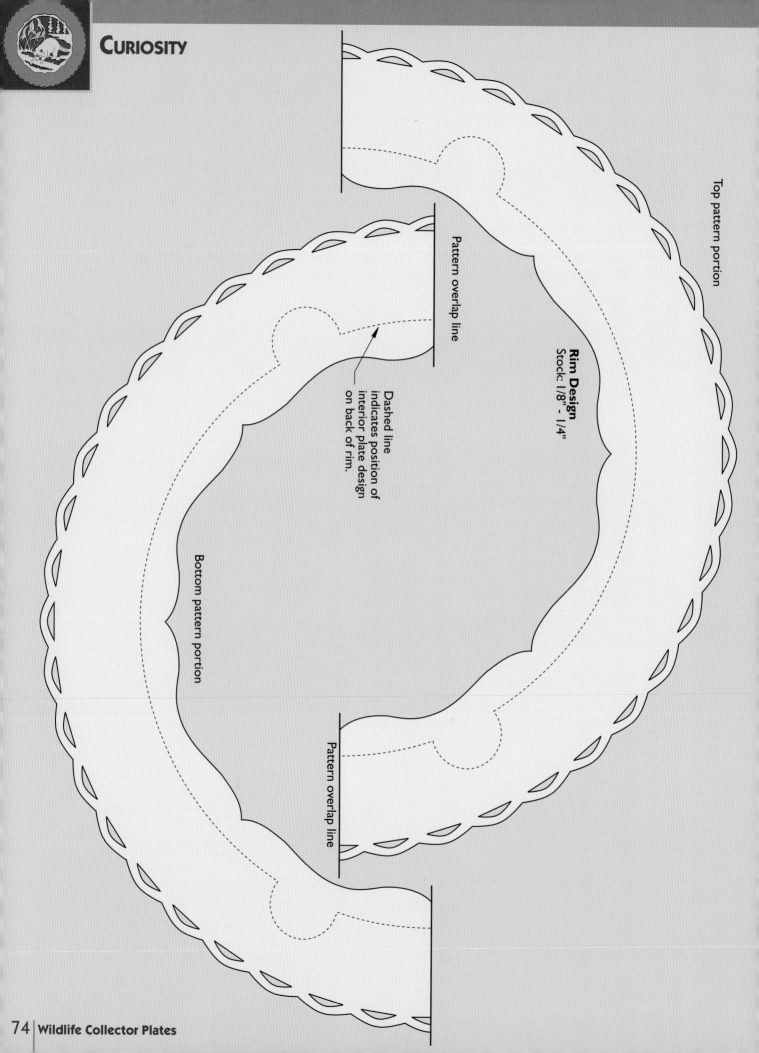

Top pattern portion

Pattern overlap line

Rim Design
Stock: 1/8" - 1/4"

Dashed line
indicates position of
interior plate design
on back of rim.

Pattern overlap line

Bottom pattern portion

Pattern overlap line

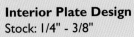

Interior Plate Design
Stock: 1/4" - 3/8"

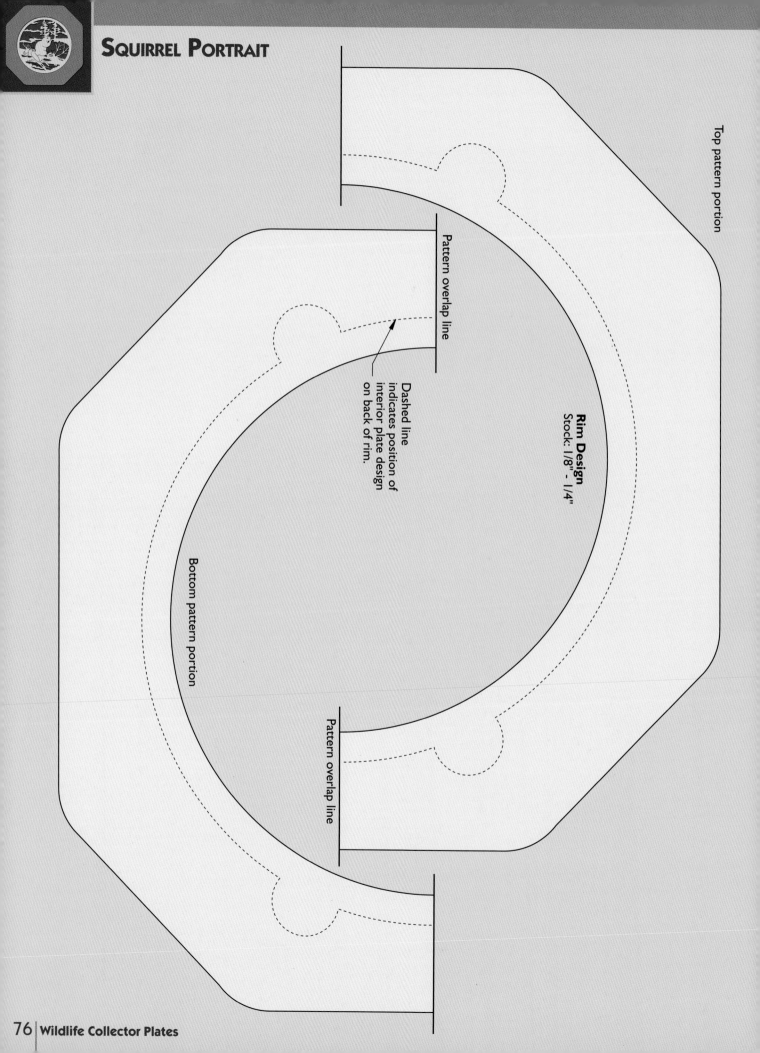

Top pattern portion

Pattern overlap line

Rim Design
Stock: 1/8" - 1/4"

Dashed line
indicates position of
interior plate design
on back of rim.

Bottom pattern portion

Pattern overlap line

Interior Plate Design
Stock: 1/4" - 3/8"

Top pattern portion

Rim Design
Stock: 1/8" - 1/4"

Pattern overlap line

Dashed line indicates
position of interior plate
design on back of rim.

Bottom pattern portion

Pattern overlap line

Interior Plate Design
Stock: 1/4" - 3/8"

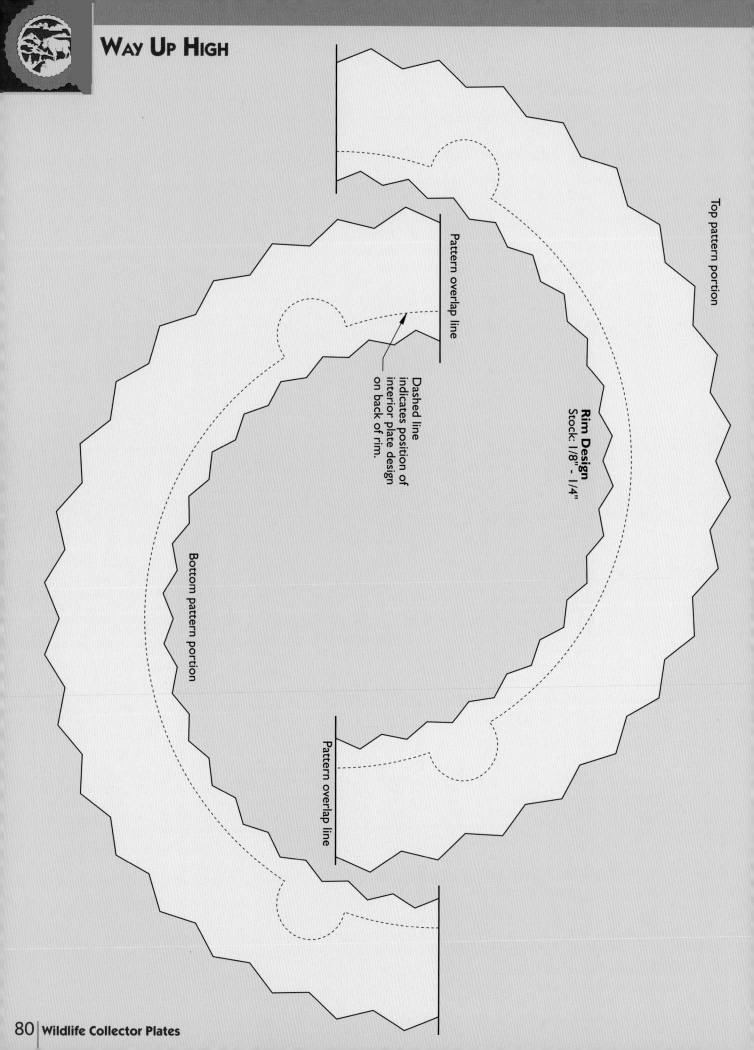

Top pattern portion

Rim Design
Stock: 1/8" - 1/4"

Pattern overlap line

Dashed line
indicates position of
interior plate design
on back of rim.

Bottom pattern portion

Pattern overlap line

Interior Plate Design
Stock: 1/4" - 3/8"

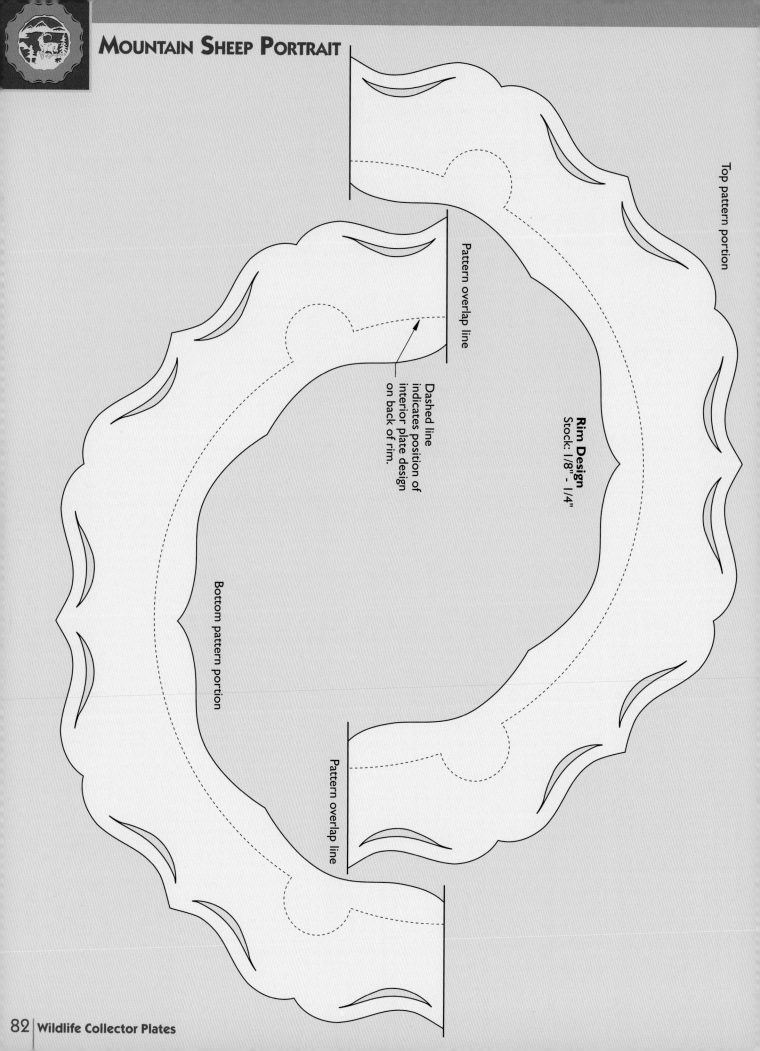

Top pattern portion

Pattern overlap line

Dashed line
indicates position of
interior plate design
on back of rim.

Rim Design
Stock: 1/8" - 1/4"

Bottom pattern portion

Pattern overlap line

Interior Plate Design
Stock: 1/4" - 3/8"

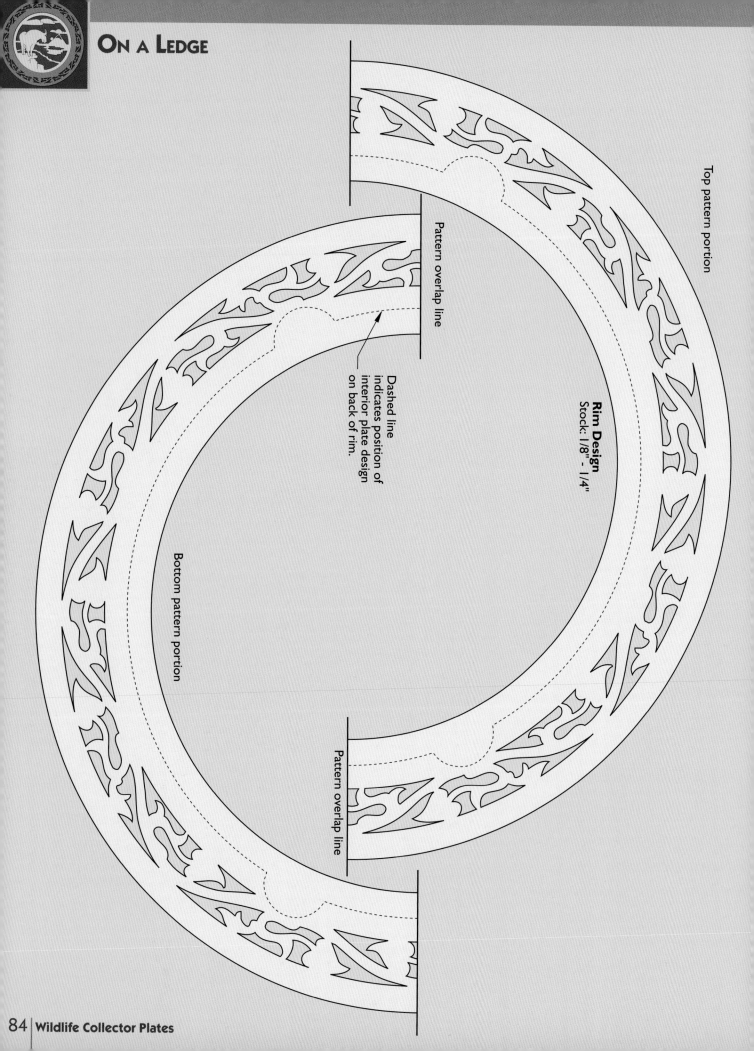

Top pattern portion

Rim Design
Stock: 1/8" - 1/4"

Pattern overlap line

Dashed line
indicates position of
interior plate design
on back of rim.

Bottom pattern portion

Pattern overlap line

Interior Plate Design
Stock: 1/4" - 3/8"

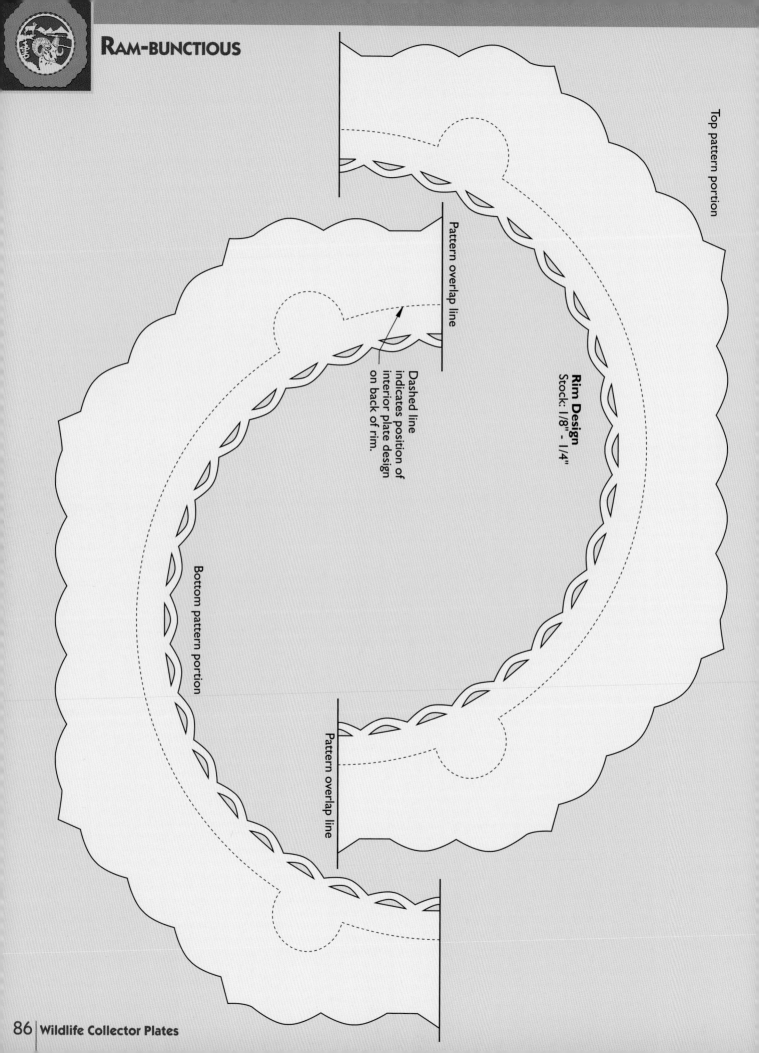

RAM-BUNCTIOUS

Top pattern portion

Pattern overlap line

Rim Design
Stock: 1/8" - 1/4"

Dashed line
indicates position of
interior plate design
on back of rim.

Pattern overlap line

Bottom pattern portion

Interior Plate Design
Stock: 1/4" - 3/8"

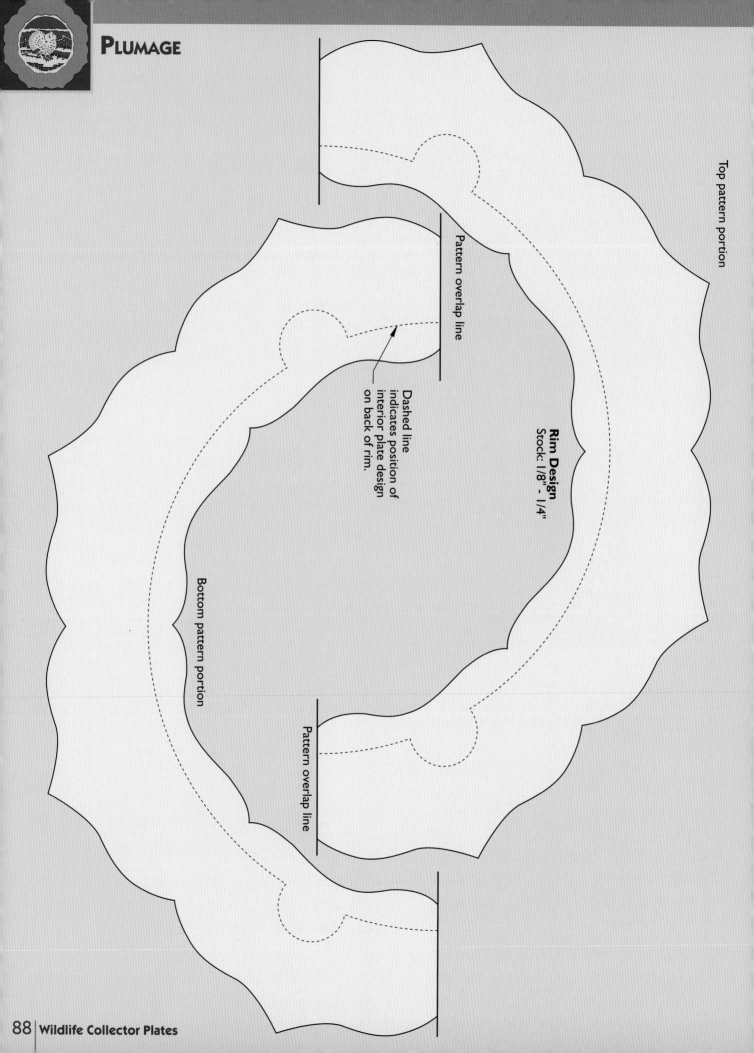

PLUMAGE

Top pattern portion

Pattern overlap line

Rim Design
Stock: 1/8" - 1/4"

Dashed line
indicates position of
interior plate design
on back of rim.

Bottom pattern portion

Pattern overlap line

Interior Plate Design
Stock: 1/4" - 3/8"

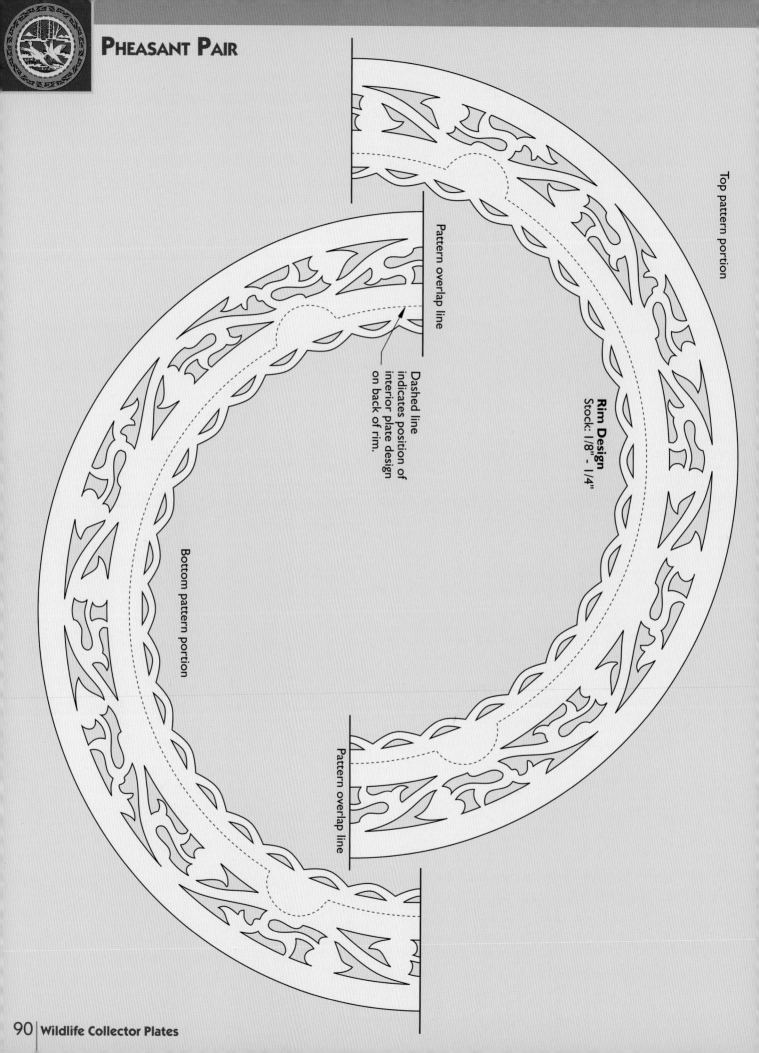

Top pattern portion

Rim Design
Stock: 1/8" - 1/4"

Pattern overlap line

Dashed line
indicates position of
interior plate design
on back of rim.

Bottom pattern portion

Pattern overlap line

Interior Plate Design
Stock: 1/4" - 3/8"

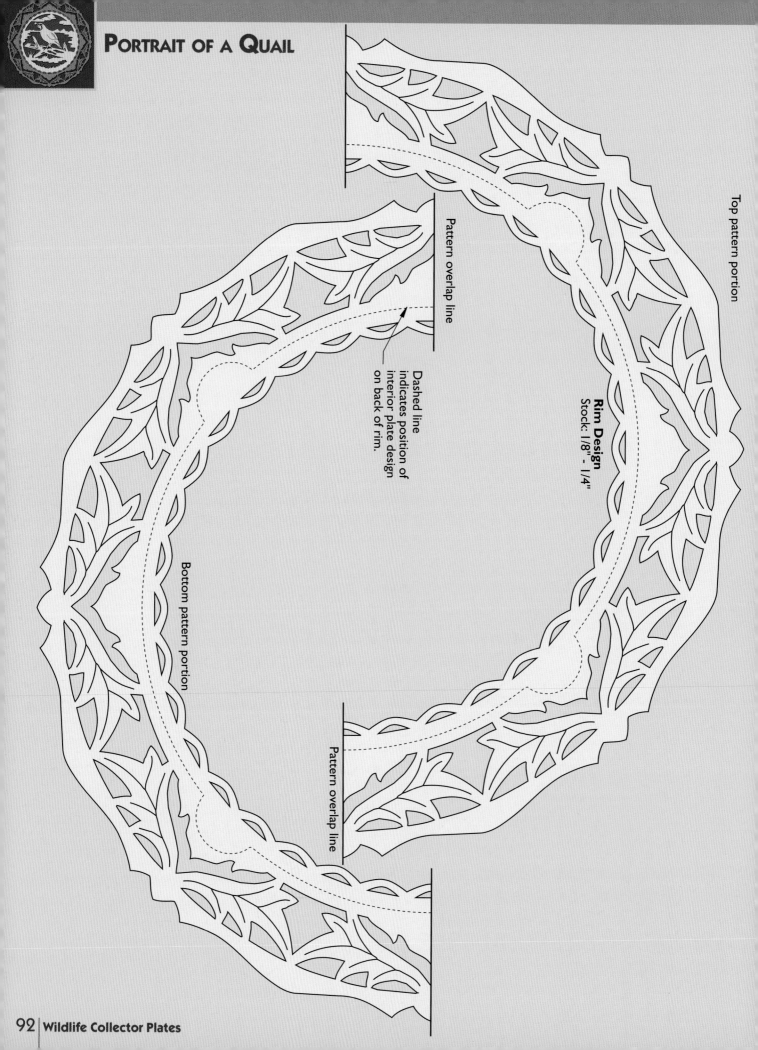

Top pattern portion

Rim Design
Stock: 1/8" - 1/4"

Pattern overlap line

Dashed line
indicates position of
interior plate design
on back of rim.

Bottom pattern portion

Pattern overlap line

Interior Plate Design
Stock: 1/4" - 3/8"

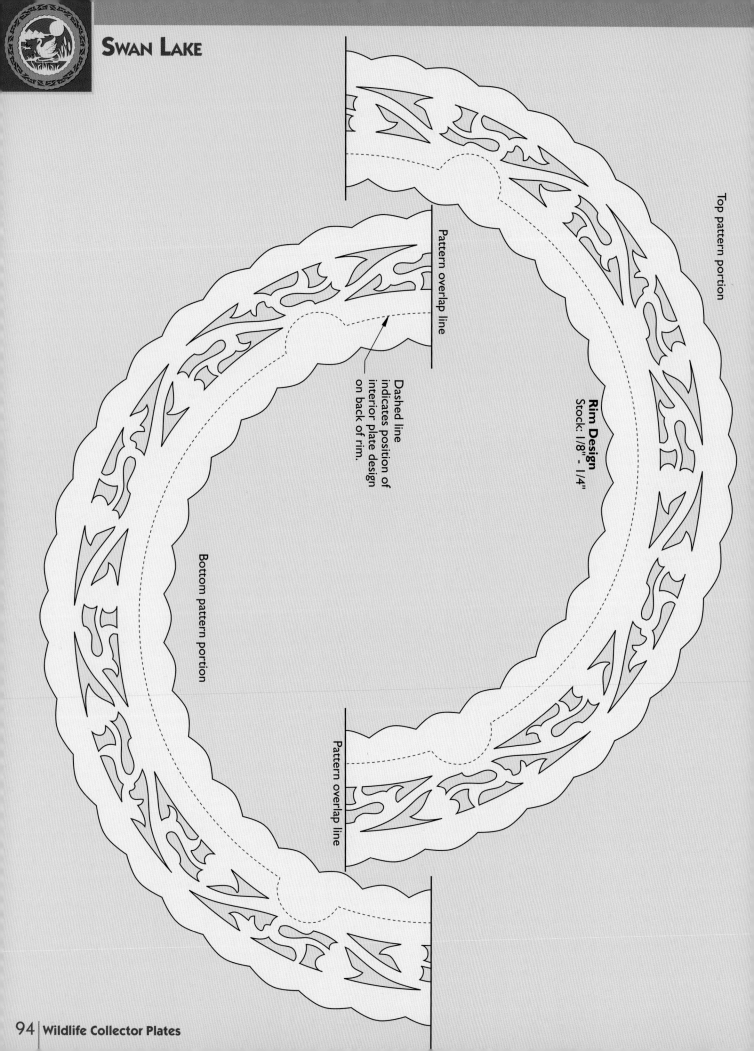

Top pattern portion

Pattern overlap line

Rim Design
Stock: 1/8" - 1/4"

Dashed line
indicates position of
interior plate design
on back of rim.

Bottom pattern portion

Pattern overlap line

Interior Plate Design
Stock: 1/4" - 3/8"

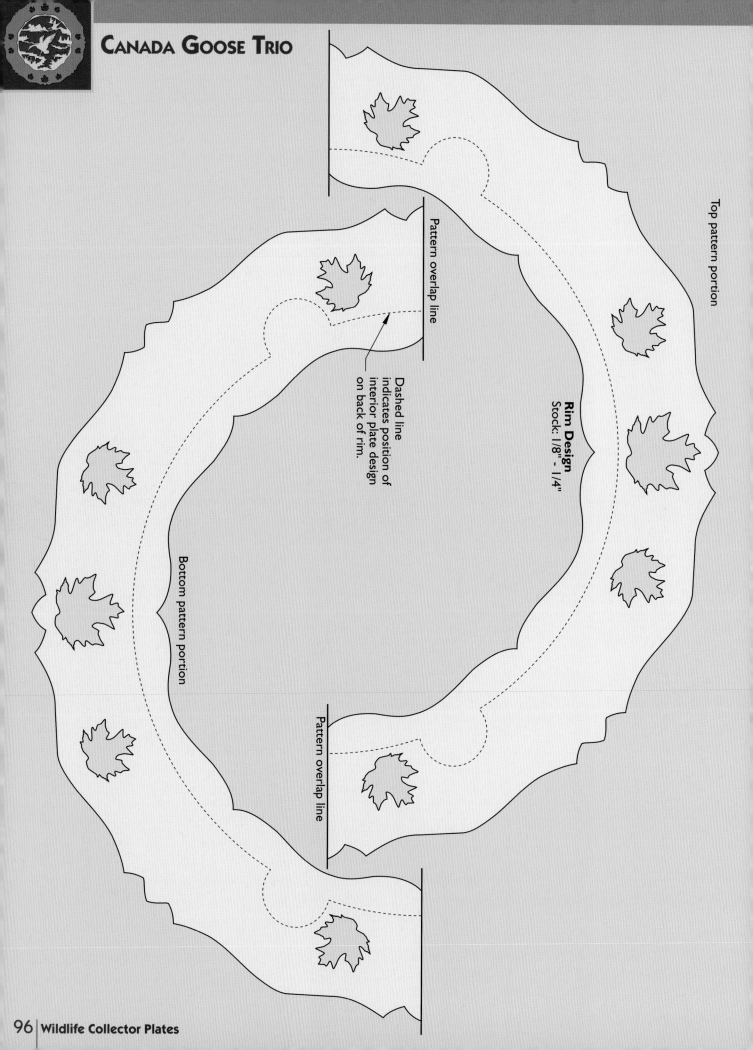

CANADA GOOSE TRIO

Top pattern portion

Pattern overlap line

Rim Design
Stock: 1/8" - 1/4"

Dashed line
indicates position of
interior plate design
on back of rim.

Bottom pattern portion

Pattern overlap line

Interior Plate Design
Stock: 1/4" - 3/8"

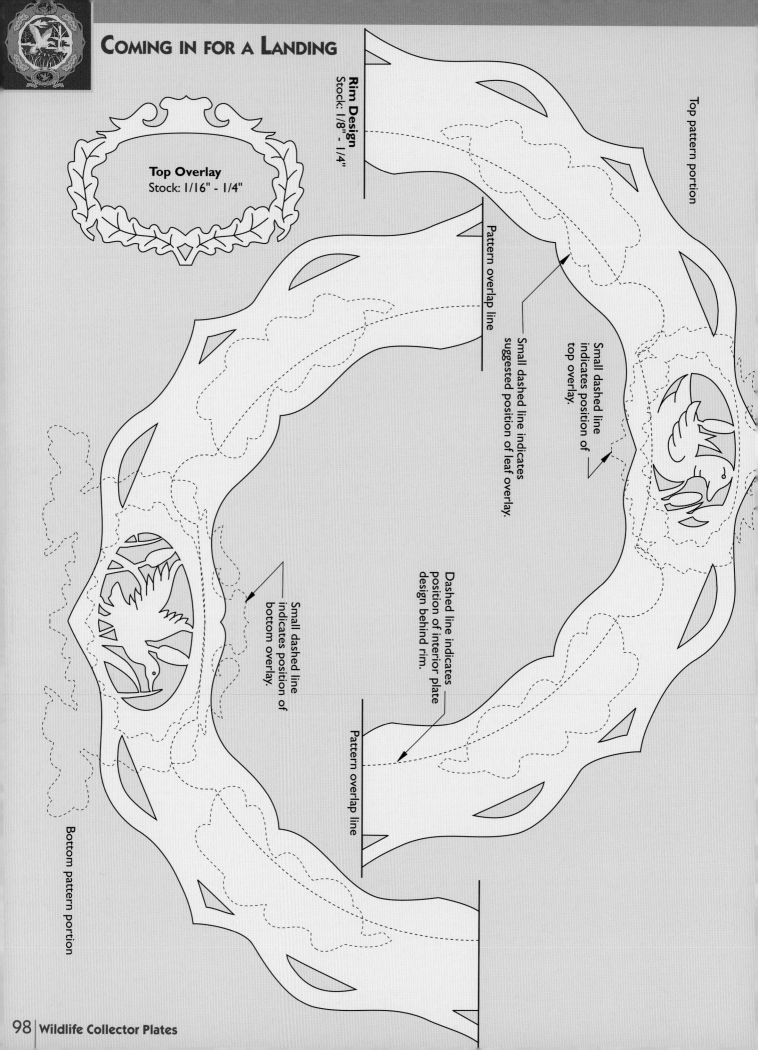

COMING IN FOR A LANDING

Rim Design
Stock: 1/8" – 1/4"

Top Overlay
Stock: 1/16" – 1/4"

Top pattern portion

Pattern overlap line

Small dashed line indicates position of top overlay.

Small dashed line indicates suggested position of leaf overlay.

Dashed line indicates position of interior plate design behind rim.

Pattern overlap line

Small dashed line indicates position of bottom overlay.

Bottom pattern portion

Interior Plate Design
Stock: 1/4" - 3/8"

Leaf Overlay
Stock: 1/16" - 1/4"

Bottom Overlay
Stock: 1/16" - 1/4"

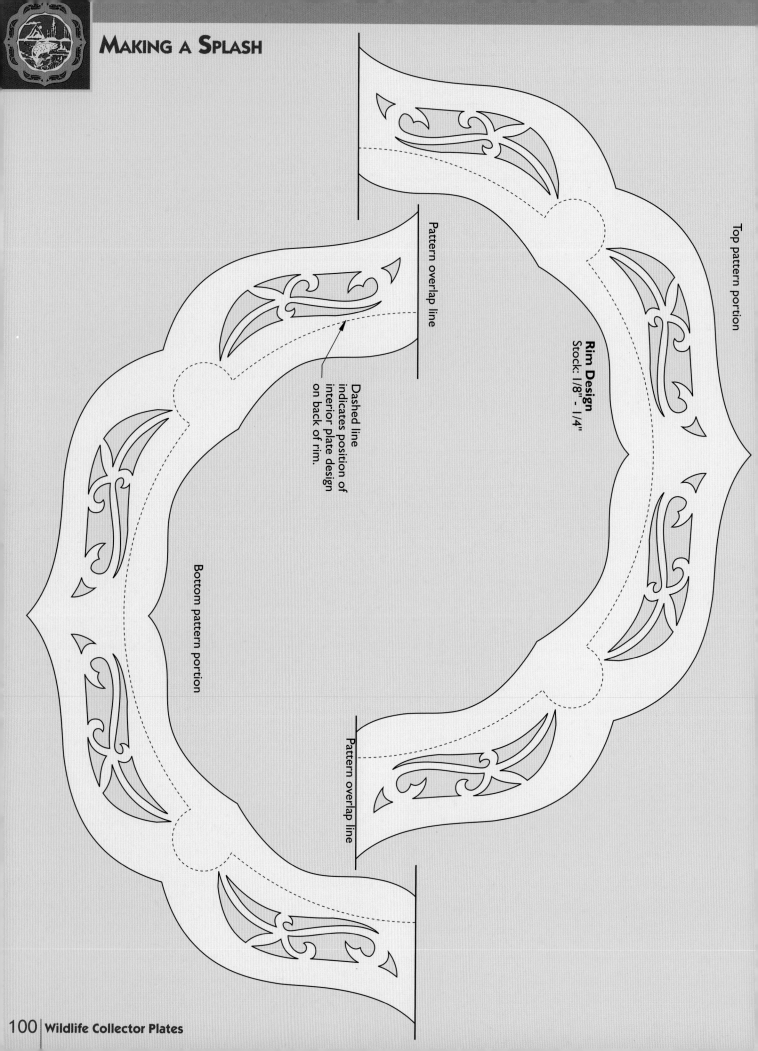

Top pattern portion

Rim Design
Stock: 1/8" - 1/4"

Pattern overlap line

Dashed line
indicates position of
interior plate design
on back of rim.

Bottom pattern portion

Pattern overlap line

Interior Plate Design
Stock: 1/4" - 3/8"

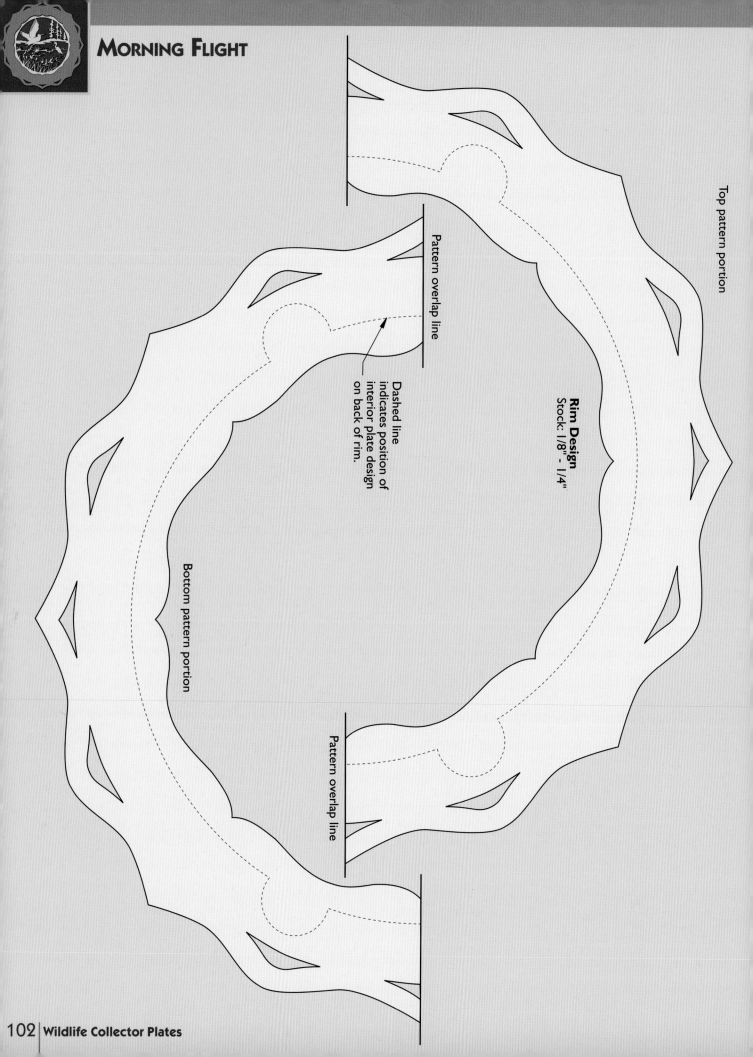

Top pattern portion

Pattern overlap line

Rim Design
Stock: 1/8" - 1/4"

Dashed line
indicates position of
interior plate design
on back of rim.

Bottom pattern portion

Pattern overlap line

Interior Plate Design
Stock: 1/4" - 3/8"

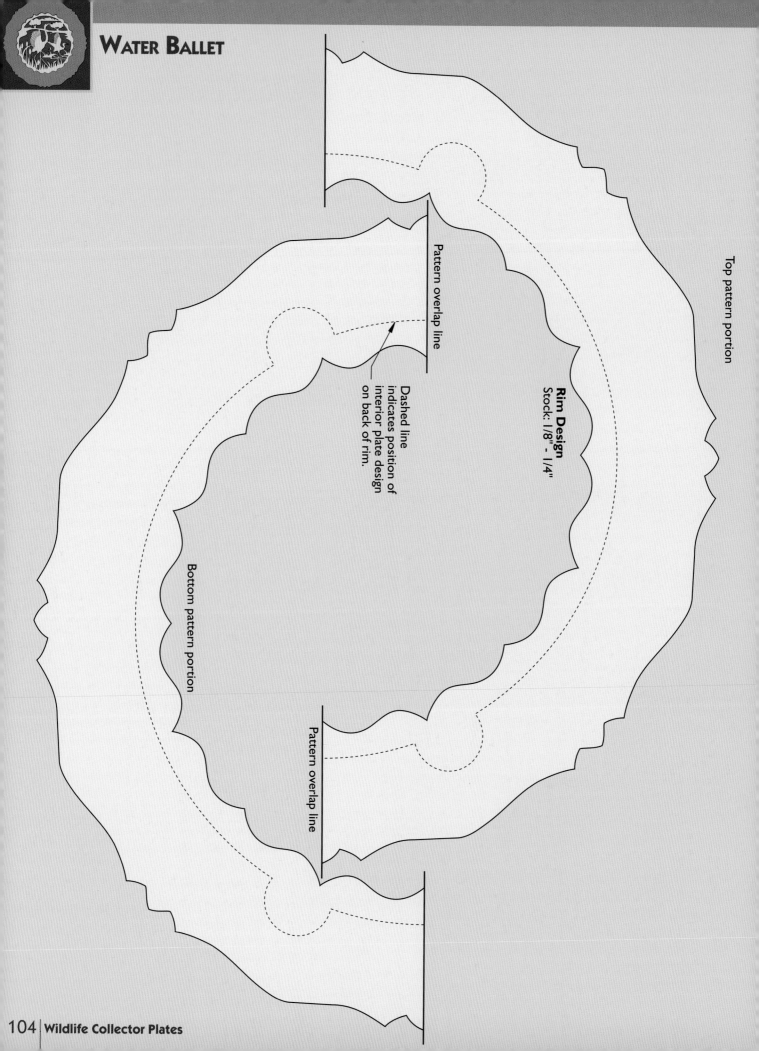

WATER BALLET

Top pattern portion

Rim Design
Stock: 1/8" - 1/4"

Pattern overlap line

Dashed line
indicates position of
interior plate design
on back of rim.

Bottom pattern portion

Pattern overlap line

Interior Plate Design
Stock: 1/4" - 3/8"

MINIPLATES — DESIGN 1

Rim Design
Stock: 1/8" - 1/4"

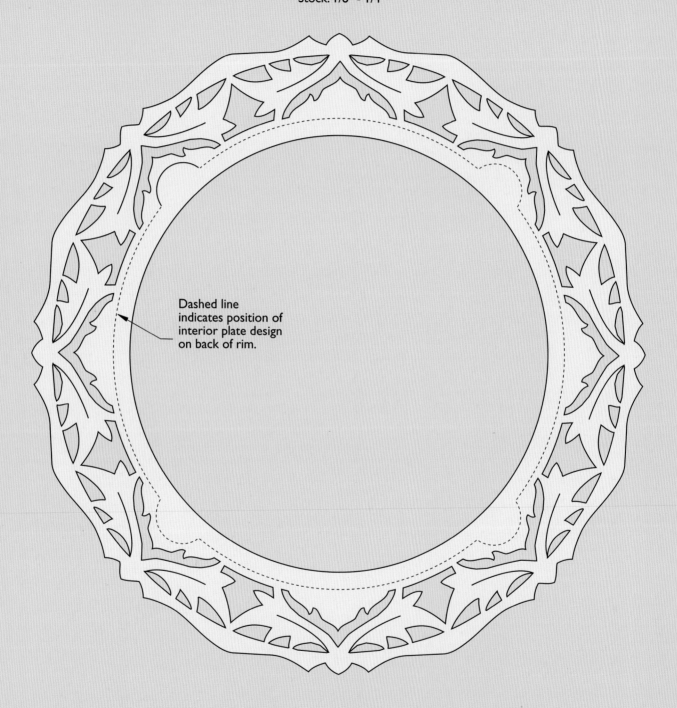

Dashed line
indicates position of
interior plate design
on back of rim.

Interior Plate Designs
Stock: 1/4" - 3/8"

Rim Design
Stock: 1/8" - 1/4"

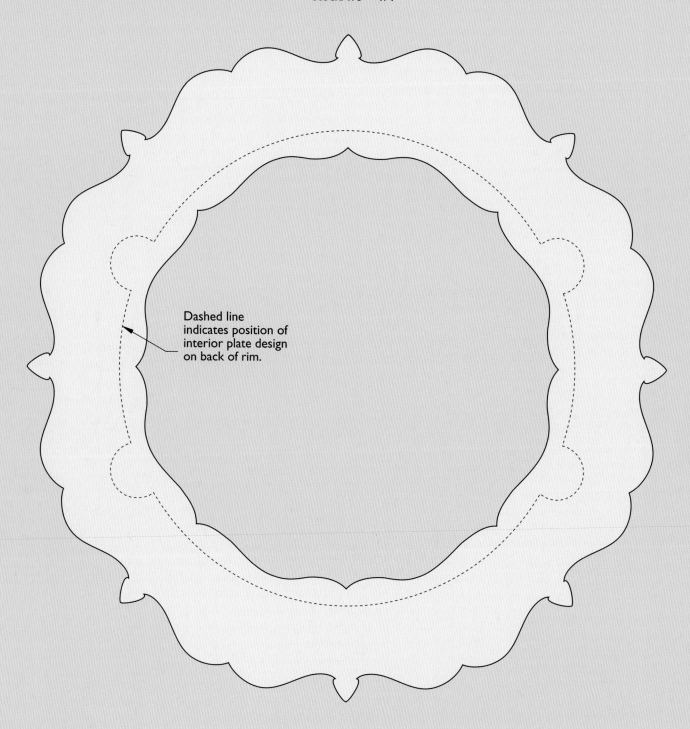

Dashed line indicates position of interior plate design on back of rim.

Interior Plate Designs
Stock: 1/4" - 3/8"

Rim Design
Stock: 1/8" - 1/4"

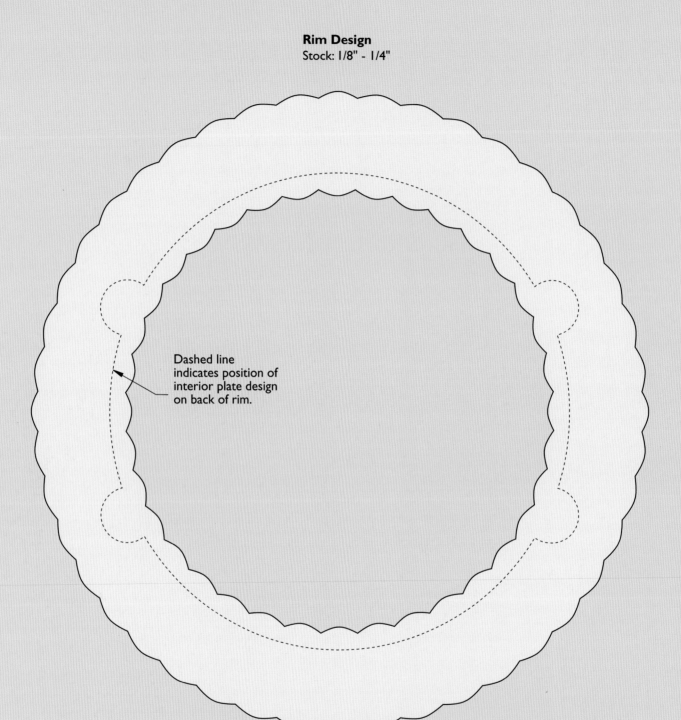

Dashed line
indicates position of
interior plate design
on back of rim.

Interior Plate Designs
Stock: 1/4" - 3/8"

Rim Design
Stock: 1/8" - 1/4"

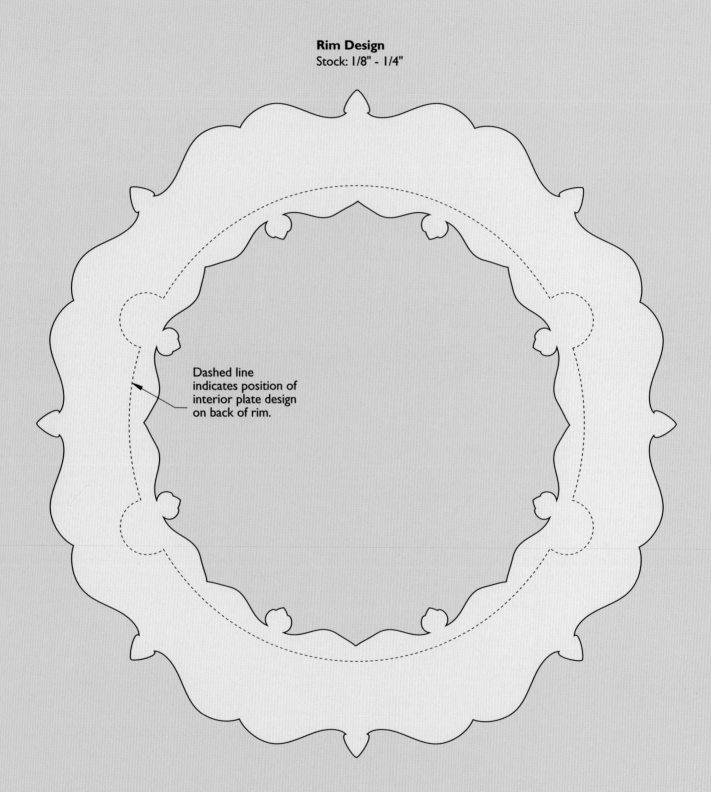

Dashed line
indicates position of
interior plate design
on back of rim.

Interior Plate Designs
Stock: 1/4" - 3/8"

MINIPLATES — DESIGN 5

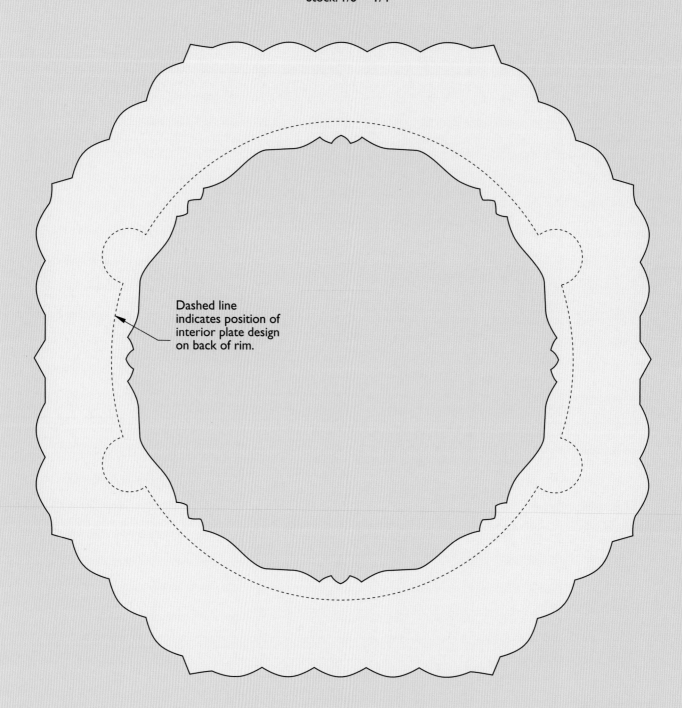

Rim Design
Stock: 1/8" - 1/4"

Dashed line
indicates position of
interior plate design
on back of rim.

Interior Plate Designs
Stock: 1/4" - 3/8"

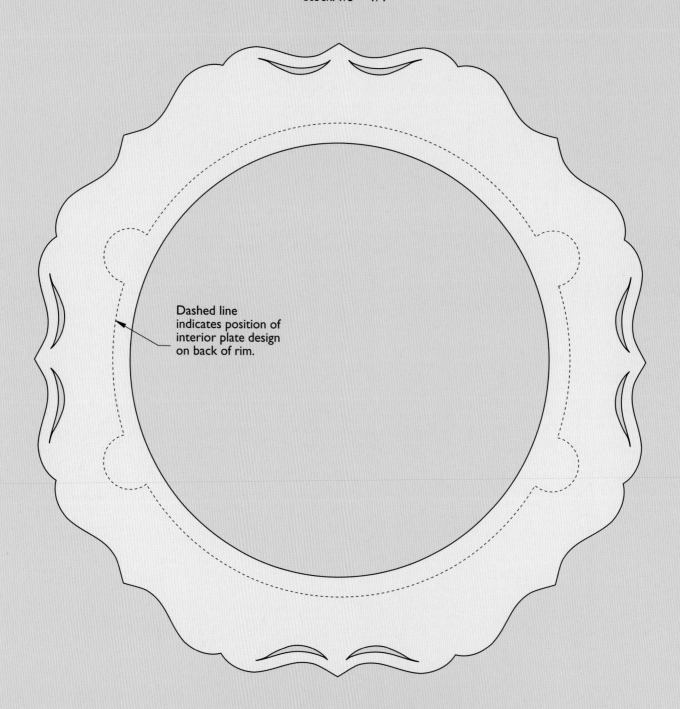

Rim Design
Stock: 1/8" - 1/4"

Dashed line
indicates position of
interior plate design
on back of rim.

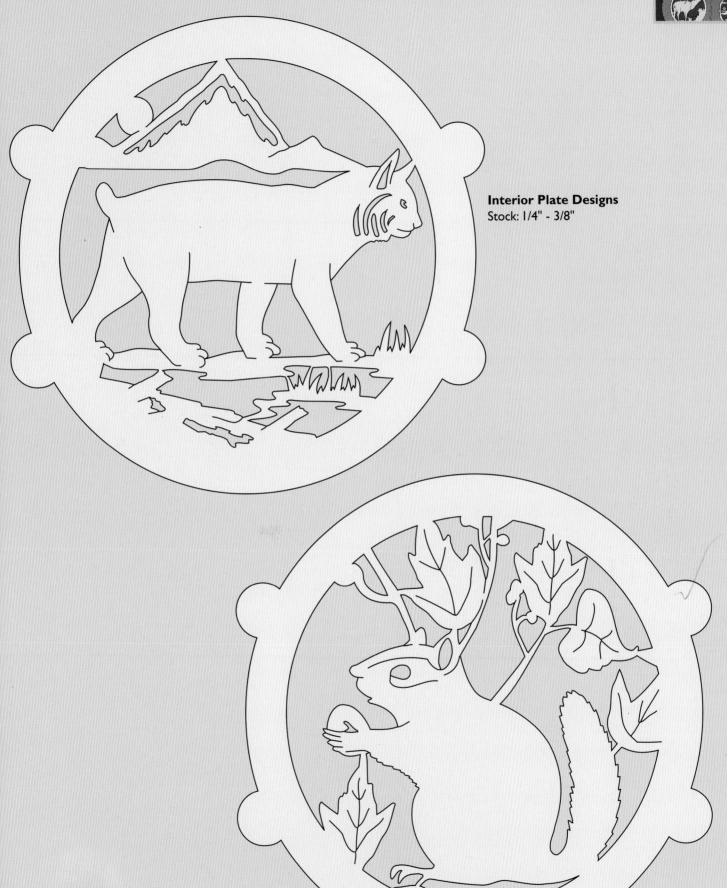

Interior Plate Designs
Stock: 1/4" - 3/8"

MINIPLATES — DESIGN 7

Rim Design
Stock: 1/8" - 1/4"

Dashed line
indicates position of
interior plate design
on back of rim.

Interior Plate Designs
Stock: 1/4" - 3/8"

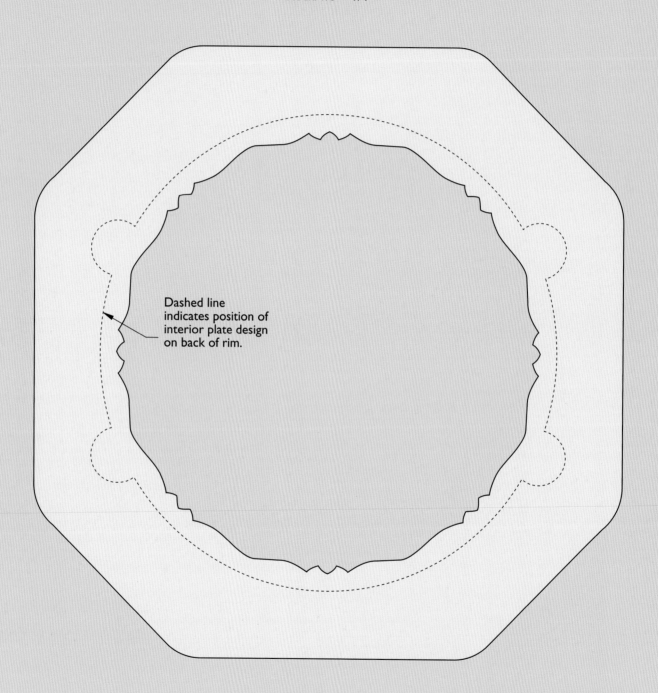

Rim Design
Stock: 1/8" - 1/4"

Dashed line
indicates position of
interior plate design
on back of rim.

Interior Plate Designs
Stock: 1/4" - 3/8"

Leaf Overlays
Enlarge/reduce overlays as desired to fit the rims of your choice. Use a contrasting wood or stain for the overlays for a more striking effect. Attach to rim with glue or silicone.

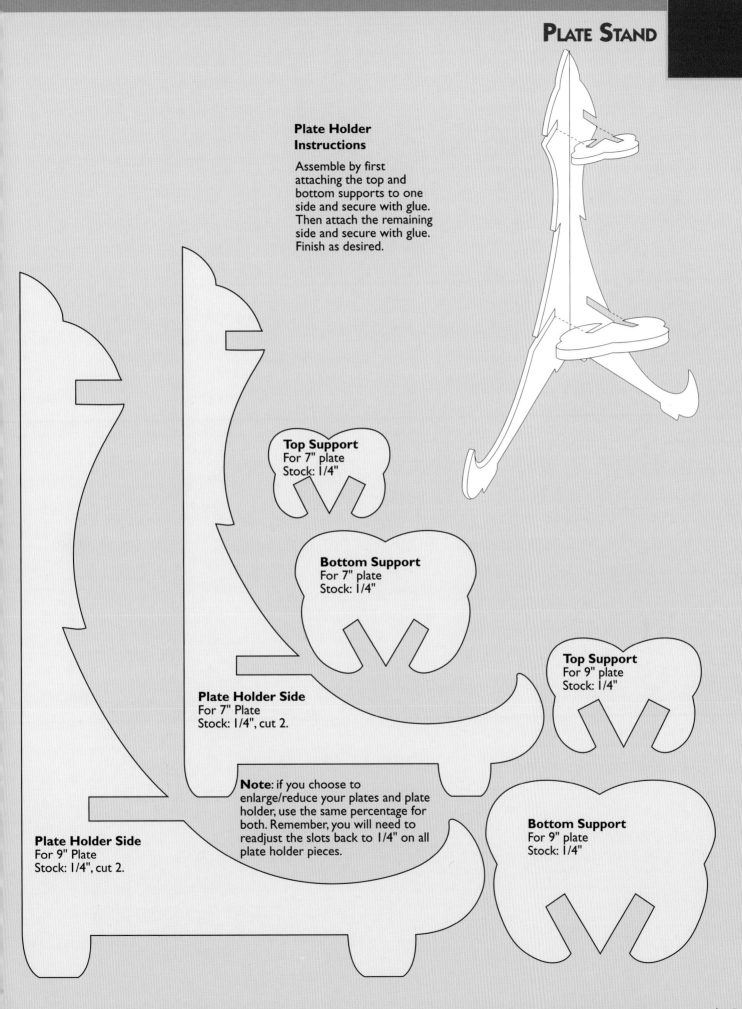

PLATE STAND

Plate Holder Instructions

Assemble by first attaching the top and bottom supports to one side and secure with glue. Then attach the remaining side and secure with glue. Finish as desired.

Top Support
For 7" plate
Stock: 1/4"

Bottom Support
For 7" plate
Stock: 1/4"

Plate Holder Side
For 7" Plate
Stock: 1/4", cut 2.

Top Support
For 9" plate
Stock: 1/4"

Plate Holder Side
For 9" Plate
Stock: 1/4", cut 2.

Note: if you choose to enlarge/reduce your plates and plate holder, use the same percentage for both. Remember, you will need to readjust the slots back to 1/4" on all plate holder pieces.

Bottom Support
For 9" plate
Stock: 1/4"

INDEX

The interior plate designs and overlays can be combined to create customized projects. To help you easily find the pieces that you need, the following index is provided for the designs and overlays in this book.

RESOURCES

To find materials and supplies for scroll sawing, contact:
The Berry Basket
PO Box 925
Centralia, WA 98531
1–800–206–9009
www.berrybasket.com

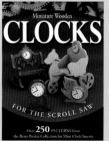